Other books by Jane Watson Hopping

The Pioneer Lady's Country Kitchen

The Pioneer Lady's Country Christmas

The Country Mothers Cookbook

The Lazy Days of Summer Cookbook

The Many Blessings Cookbook

The Pioneer Lady's
Hearty Winter Cookbook

The Pioneer Lady's
Hearty Winter Cookbook

A Treasury of Old-Fashioned Foods
and Fond Memories

JANE WATSON HOPPING

Villard   New York

LIBRARY OF CONGRESS CATALOGING-IN-PUBLICATION DATA
Hopping, Jane Watson.
The pioneer lady's hearty winter cookbook/Jane Watson Hopping
p.   cm.
ISBN 0-679-41476-2 (acid-free paper)
1. Cookery, American. 2. Winter.
TX715.H7867   1996
641.5´64—dc20   93-33540

Manufactured in the United States of America on acid-free paper

9 8 7 6 5 4 3 2

First Edition

DESIGNED BY BARBARA MARKS

For All Those Who Love Midwinter

Then blow, Winds, blow!
And rave and shriek,
And snarl and snow,
Till your breath grows weak—
While here in my room
I'm as snugly shut
As a glad little worm
In the heart of a nut!

—From *Winter Fantasy*, James Whitcomb Riley

Acknowledgments

With each new book, I grow more aware that my writing has been influenced by those who with enthusiasm share their Pioneer Lady's cookbooks with friends, thus introducing them to others. I am touched by those who give my various books as gifts to grandmothers, mothers, wives, sisters, daughters, and friends.

Thus it gives me great pleasure to be able to thank all of those above for their support. And it pleases me to let them know that I am always encouraged by their response to my work. They are my inspiration and the source of inspiration for books yet to come.

Many thanks to Alvin Reiss, who shares his poetry with me, and also to Sheila and Patricia Parrish Kuhn, who share their talents.

Sincerely,

JANE WATSON HOPPING

Contents

xiv

Contents

Beautiful Sunshine

It's raining outside, it's snowing some too,
and I'm stuck inside with nothing to do
but sit by the window and watch it come down.
The baby is sleeping. I can't make a sound.
Wait! There is the sun. I can go out and splash
in the puddles that are all about.

When it's all said, and when it's all done,
It's nice to have rain,
but it's great to have sun!

—Barbara Hopping

Introduction: A Quietness on the Land

As brilliant fall days fade into winterized landscapes, I find myself staying longer at the desk, capturing visions of falling snow on a windless night, warm fires, and lively conversations—the essence of midwinter.

Daily the chapters evolve into a tapestry. The first threads are laid down throughout December, gently touching the holy days of Christmas, turning on past the New Year into cold but lovely January, stopping to pick up the delicate white, purple, and yellow colors of February's crocus corners, celebrating the first raucous days of spring in March, and ending with enchanted April.

Outside my window, giant snowflakes casually begin to float over the farm, dropping an ermine blanket over fence posts, piles of lumber, barn roofs, and tall evergreens. As the days grow shorter, I spend more time indoors, writing text, gathering and testing recipes full of simple and inexpensive ingredients. Some special goodies or rib-sticking dishes are family recipes handed down and shared. Most are comfort foods, the favorite family fare!

Rain or snow on the roof, and winds that whip around corners to ring the chimes, bring to mind memories of childhood: skating on a frozen pond, throwing a snowball, watching snowbirds dart here and there only to land on a snow-covered branch or a barren tree.

I think of Mama, who baked cookies in our old wood-burning cookstove. We could barely wait to eat them. Mama brought tall glasses of icy-cold milk to go with the cookies. She taught us to cool our fingertips by wrapping our hands around the glass of milk. When supper was ready, she would sit down by our cozy kitchen fire and rock the baby, Sheila, in her lap and let me sit at her feet or hang over her knee. "Listen!" she would tell me. "Listen to the tap of rain on the roof and water dripping off the eaves, the winter world is beginning to thaw!"

Then Grandpa and Daddy would come stomping up onto the porch, wiping mud off their boots. Mama had their coffee ready and a generous plate of cookies set out on our old kitchen table. Grandpa and Daddy would eat handfuls of cookies and tell us women that supper could wait.

> *The year's at the spring*
> *And the day's at the morn,*
> *God's in his Heaven—*
> *All's right with the world.*

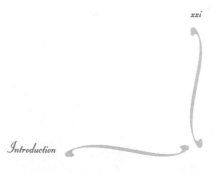

Winter Day

Oh, what a lovely day to go
Walking through the feathery snow,
The exquisite carven leaves of snow.

There is a wood path I shall follow
Up a hill and down a hollow,
A path that winds through a grove of firs
And spruces etched with gossamers
Of frosted white and needled green,
With little golden cones between.
And the little path is intimate
With the pheasant's and the squirrel's estate;
The mullein candles' sun-tipped spires
Glitter and gleam with enchanted fires;
Goldenrod plumes and Queen Anne's lace
Are crystal blooms of fabulous race.
And the pungent fragrance! Who can distill
The perfume of a snow-roofed hill?
Oh, what a lovely day to go
Climbing through the falling snow.
Here on this hill slope I shall find
Health for my body and peace for my mind.

—Marion Doyle, *Best Loved Unity Poems*

The Pioneer Lady's
Hearty Winter Cookbook

A Wayside Shrine and an Altar in the Snow

One cold, blustery winter day before Christmas, Uncle Bud and his friend George Hathaway decided to trudge through the woods behind George and Mary's house to look for a Christmas tree. They gathered a few berries for the women who were decorating the house, put a few small pinecones in their pockets, and carried in their hands a few giant ones. They decided to climb over the woodlot fence and return home by way of the lane, or as George's family called it, the road.

About a quarter of a mile from home, they came upon a pile of rocks and punky logs stacked up like a small building and covered with snow. George thought gypsies might have camped in the woods before the storm. Uncle Bud thought it looked like the work of children at play. Then George spied a small piece of paper. The two of them opened it and read it:

> Dear Lord, thank you for this fine year, thank you for Daddy and Mama, my picky sisters, and Uncle Bud. And thank you for Christmas time because people act nice to each other and it's so much fun.
>
> P.S. I will gladly play Joseph in the school Christmas pageant, and I will sing holy songs in the choir at church.
>
> George II, Tommy, Bill, Jack, and young Bud

All of this brought tears to the eyes of their fathers!

A Sleigh Ride to the Timber and Back to the Barn

I long for the days on grandmother's farm
sleigh rides to the timber and back to the barn.
For her hot baked bread and applebutter spread
the cold winter nights in her four-poster bed.

Rising up with the rooster, the cattle to feed
the corn to shuck and the bread to knead.
Then when chores were a' finished on time and just right
to her lap we would hurry for her tales of delight.

Quick up the worn stairway, we'd climb for our naps
then back down for supper, not long before taps.
At our chairs we would kneel on a hard wooden floor
while grandfather with Bible, our Lord did implore.

—DAILY BLESSINGS, Patricia Parish Kuhn

Well into her old age, Mother recalled trips in the family's farm wagon across country to visit older relatives and friends. She never let us forget that strong families are nurturers of mankind, and that from such family bonding there flows to the young ideals, morals, values, and much more.

5

An Overnight Stay at My Grandparents' Farm

How fortunate are children who live closely bonded to their family, who throughout childhood know the pleasure of staying awhile with grandparents and seeing themselves in ancient love-filled eyes. Children whose aunties try to feed them three or four times a day; young

uncles who say, "Go ask Grandpa for a ball and I'll play catch with you!" Or, if young, having the delight of older cousins swing them on the old tire swing.

I particularly enjoyed old uncles who told family stories.

Jane Watson Hopping

Granny's Best-Ever Brown Bread

MAKES 3 LOAVES

Old-time women had special recipes like this simple staple bread that they counted on. My grandmother baked nine loaves each Saturday to go along with her hurry-up soda and baking powder biscuits.

2 tablespoons granulated yeast
³/₄ cup warm water (105° to 115°F)
2 cups milk
¹/₄ cup (¹/₂ stick) butter or margarine, at room temperature, plus 2 or more tablespoons (optional) for brushing tops of loaves after baking

3 tablespoons sugar
4 teaspoons salt
5¹/₂ cups all-purpose flour
2 cups unsifted whole-wheat flour

Dissolve the yeast in the warm water; let sit until mixture foams.

In a large saucepan, heat the milk and the ¹/₄ cup butter to lukewarm; stir in the sugar and salt. Add the yeast mixture. Mix until well blended, then pour into a large bowl. Add flour, 1 cup at a time, begining with white flour, then whole-wheat; beat well. Stir in as much additional flour as needed to make a stiff dough.

Turn out onto lightly floured surface. Knead until smooth. Place in a bread bowl that has been thoroughly washed, dried, and greased. Cover and let rise until double in bulk. Divide into 3 parts. Shape into 3 loaves, place in greased 9-by-5-by-2¹/₂-inch loaf pans, and let rise again until doubled. (To test, touch the dough. If an impression remains when touched, the dough has doubled in bulk.)

While dough is rising, preheat oven to 375°F. Bake until well risen, lightly browned, and firm to the touch. To test for doneness, lift loaf. If it's golden brown on the bottom and turns easily out of the pan, it's done.

Remove all loaves from pans and place on a wire rack to cool. If desired, while the loaves are still hot, brush tops with 2 or more tablespoons butter or margarine.

7

Grandpa's Favorite Oven Stew

MAKES 6 TO 8
SERVINGS

Our mother seldom worked off the homeplace. During the spring and summer, she raised laying hens, sold eggs for pin money, and tended a large garden, and from April to October she milked two or three cows and sold the milk. She also bought property and sold it, owned two rentals which, by herself, she roofed, painted, and wall-papered.

In addition she baked bread and took care of her aging father, her hard-working husband, and my sister and me. We have often talked about the high quality of life she provided for us.

She often made oven stew using meat from the animals she had raised for market, as her mother had done when there were ten in the family to feed. She was generous but frugal. For example, she saved bones from the steaks she fried for supper, and made broth from them for other dishes.

Give her of the fruit of her hands;
and let her own works praise her in the gates.

Proverbs 31:31

3 tablespoons margarine	Salt and freshly ground black pepper
1/2 large onion, peeled and chopped	1/2 cup celery, diced
1 clove garlic, peeled and crushed	1 large carrot, peeled and cubed
1 1/2 pounds lean stew beef, cut into 1- to 2-inch cubes	3 medium potatoes, peeled and diced
1/2 cup flour	2 cups Homemade Beef Broth (recipe follows)

Preheat oven to 350°F.

In a large skillet, heat margarine; sauté onion and garlic until clear; remove from skillet and put in a small bowl. Shake the cubes of meat in the flour and a small amount of salt and pepper in a small paper bag until coated. Add to the skillet and brown in the hot margarine (add a little more margarine if needed, but not too much or it will make the stew greasy).

Jane Watson Hopping

Layer the rare meat, onions, garlic, celery, carrots, and potatoes in a large covered baking dish, salting and peppering as needed between layers. Pour the broth over the meat and vegetables, and add water as needed so that the vegetables and meat are almost covered. Cover the casserole, and bake until the meat and potatoes are tender, about 45 minutes.

Homemade Beef Broth — MAKES 2 CUPS OR MORE

One or more pounds beef bones with a small amount of meat clinging to them

$^1/_2$ teaspoon salt

1 bay leaf
1 stalk celery, with leaves left on
1 whole clove

Place the bones in a large saucepan; cover with cold water and add salt. Bring to a boil. Cover and simmer over medium heat until the meat falls off the bones and broth reduces to half, 1 hour or more. Remove from heat, let cool until the fat rises, and remove it from broth. Heat clear broth to boiling. Add bay leaf, celery, and clove. Simmer 10 to 15 minutes. Strain broth into a small saucepan; discard vegetables and seasoning agents.

Measure broth. Two cups will be needed for recipe above. Reserve remaining clear broth for soup stock.

The Pioneer Lady's Hearty Winter Cookbook

Old-Fashioned Apple-Butter Spread

MAKES ABOUT 4 QUARTS

When I was a little girl, we went every fall to Apple Hill to pick apples or to buy prepicked apples for winter. Mama always bargained with the farmer for "seconds," apples that were small or blemished. She would say to our father, "These will do fine for applesauce and apple butter."

I had to wait in the car with my little sister, but as soon as the full gunnysacks were put in the back seat and the trunk of the car, we were given apples to munch on.

12 pounds apples (Rome Beauty, Golden Delicious, Jonathan, late McIntosh, and Spitzenberg)	6 cups sugar
1 gallon sweet apple cider	1 tablespoon ground cinnamon
	1 teaspoon ground cloves

Wash, pare, core, and slice apples. In a large saucepan or kettle, cook apples in cider until soft, 15 to 20 minutes or more. Press through a sieve or food mill. Over low heat, boil until thick enough to heap on a spoon, another 10 minutes. Stir constantly to prevent apple butter from sticking to the bottom of the pan. Remove from heat. Add sugar and spices; blend well. Return apple mixture to the heat. Cook over low heat an additional 5 to 8 minutes.

Remove from heat. Pour while hot into hot sterilized pint canning jars. Meanwhile, heat the lids in boiling water, wipe down tops and sides of jars, then screw on sterilized rings. Process jars in boiling water bath for 10 minutes.

Jane Watson Hopping

About a Road That Winds Through Quiet Woods

When I was just a little girl, only about six years old, my mother would hold baby Sheila in her lap and I would sit at her feet while she talked to us about love that has no ending. She would sing to us old gospel songs. When baby Sheila went to sleep, Mother would tell me that the words of the song held a message for us all, that Christ teaches us through faith and duty, through love for ourselves and others, how to live a rich and fulfilling life.

Sing them over again to me, Wonderful Words of Life;
Let me more of their beauty see, wonderful Words of Life.
Words of life and beauty, Teach me faith and duty:
Beautiful words, wonderful words, Wonderful Words of Life.

The Pioneer Lady's Hearty Winter Cookbook

Courtesy of Esther Posley Meekins

From *Little Woman*

My little woman, of you I sing
With a fervor all divine,—
For I know the clasp of the hands that cling
So closely here in mine.

Though the rosy palms I used to press
Are faded and worn with care,
And tremulous is the old caress
That nestles in my hair,—

Your heart to me is a changeless page;
I have read it bit by bit,
From the dawn of love to the dusk of age,—
And the tale is Holy Writ.

—James Whitcomb Riley

Jane Watson Hopping

From the Dawn of Love to the Dusk of Age

A true love story, one that speaks of lifetime commitment, is rare indeed.

Once during a winter storm, Mama told us about her friends Albert and Ellie, who had no children and who were passionately loyal to each other. Throughout the many years she had known them, she never heard either one speak harshly to the other. Aunt Clary swore that when they disagreed, Albert and Ellie spoke softly until the misunderstanding was resolved.

As Ellie aged and became more fragile, Albert helped her with the cooking, sweeping, and washing. He bought a new rocking chair for her, which he moved about so that they could visit while he worked and he could be certain that she was comfortable.

Sometimes, when my life and relationships seem a bit hectic, I find a quiet place on the farm where I can ponder life's wonders. I often recall Albert and Ellie's lack of material goods, their loving kindness to each other, and the richness of their life together.

Simple
Vegetable Soup

∿

During the mid-thirties, older folk were sometimes short on money, food, and heat. Young women, like Mama and Effie, went regularly to their homes, taking freshly baked bread, meat left over from a Sunday dinner, milk, and eggs. Sometimes they brought a stewing hen and enough eggs to make noodles.

Effie, a strong and kind Christian woman, believed firmly that one should "Open thy mouth, judge righteously, and plead the cause of the poor and needy." As long as she lived, she spoke out for those whose lives had gone astray, were down on their luck or lonely.

1 tablespoon butter or margarine (Great-Grandma preferred butter)
2 large carrots, peeled and diced
2 stalks tender celery, chopped
4 cups chicken broth, homemade or store-bought
1 cup cauliflower florets
1/2 cup green peas

1/2 cup green beans
2 large tomatoes, peeled, seeded, and cut into 1-inch cubes
Salt and freshly ground black pepper to taste
1 tablespoon fresh basil, finely chopped

Heat butter in a large saucepan. Sauté carrots and celery in sizzling butter until softened but not browned, about 3 minutes. Meanwhile, bring chicken broth to a boil. Add the sautéed vegetables to the chicken broth, add cauliflower, and simmer 15 minutes. Add peas, green beans, and tomatoes, and simmer 10 minutes more; then add salt and pepper and minced basil, as desired.

Serve in deep soup bowls, with Aunt Esther's Whole-Wheat Bread (page 198).

Jane Watson Hopping

Jewel Faces

There were two lovely faces that I saw
Set in white frames of softly waving hair,
They touched my heart with something kin to awe,
For more than youthful prettiness was there;
Reflections as from inner placid pools
Seemed shining in those eyes so calm and cool,
As though life, passing, left no outer sign,
Save writing noble thoughts in every line.

And then, unnumbered faces in review
Passed by, and brought the thought of gems to me;
For some we deeply prize a life-time through,
And others glance at once—and carelessly;
Some have a diamond's hard and brilliant shine,
Like pearls are others, pale and pure and cold;
Some have the ruby's color—deep as wine—
And some are opals, flaming, bright and bold.

And those I saw—the two sweet faces there—
Set in white frames of softly waving hair,
Not soon shall I forget, for those—ah, those
Were cameos!

—Grace E. Hall, *Patchwork*

Cameos
Rare

Often on rainy or snowy days, Mother used to tell us about the old folk, ancient family members like Aunt Clary and her friend Floyd. Sometimes she talked about Aunt Alice, and Aunt Fanny, but for the most part, she talked about Aunt Clary, whom she so fondly recalled. Mother's gentle memories filled our minds with visions of days gone by, leaving us with a deep understanding and fondness for family members gone but never forgotten.

To this day, I can visualize Aunt Clary, whose once-great crown of chestnut hair was thinned by time and turned to silver with age. Mama, who loved her great-aunt, affectionately spoke of Aunt Clary's aged beauty, her soft wrinkled face and bright intelligent eyes, and her kind and gentle ways. Mother, with tears misting in her eyes, told us that Aunt Clary was a rare cameo, indeed.

Floyd was like a companion piece to Aunt

16

Jane Watson Hopping

Clary, his still-handsome face etched with lines that revealed the beauty of his soul. He was forever looking after her, making sure she did not suffer want, bringing her sweet fruits off his trees, and easing her loneliness. In the end, he was the one gently holding her hand.

Inner Placid Pools

Our old folk have a gentle acceptance of life as it is and has been—an acceptance that seems to flow from some inner placid pool. They have a soft, loving way with the little ones that promises them a life worth living. Through their actions, the elders share the belief that our children are the future.

All the younger folk in the family have the same respect for the elderly. When my father grew older, Mother, Sheila, and I intuitively knew that some of his strength and character had become ours. We were content when he didn't do anything other than sit in his chair and doze. His presence was enough.

Mama's Diced Chicken and Homemade Noodles

When I was a child, Mama often made this dish. Early in the morning, she made the noodles and then hung them up to dry. First, she made the dough and rolled it very thin. She then laid a clean broom handle over the back of two kitchen chairs, and draped a clean cotton cloth over the broom handle. This became the rack over which she stretched her noodle dough to dry.

Often when they were still a bit tender, she rolled the noodles up like a jelly roll and, with a sharp knife, cut them into narrow strips. She then added them to the pot of chicken and broth.

3-pound chicken, precooked, skin and fat removed, diced (reserve 4 or more cups of the chicken broth)
1 cup diced celery
1/3 cup finely minced onion
1 teaspoon salt
1/4 teaspoon freshly ground black pepper

1/2 teaspoon dried thyme, crumbled
1/4 teaspoon granulated garlic, or one small clove
Mama's Homemade Noodles (recipe follows)

In a large soup pot or Dutch oven, combine diced chicken, celery, onion, salt, pepper, thyme, and garlic. Pour reserved chicken broth over the above combined ingredients. Add water as needed to make 2 quarts. Taste and adjust seasoning if you wish. Bring to a boil, lower heat, and cook until vegetables are tender, 15 to 20 minutes. Add dried, uncooked noodles to boiling chicken broth. Over medium heat, boil lightly until noodles are tender, 15 minutes.

Serve in a large soup bowl with freshly grated Celeriac, Carrot, and Apple Salad (page 20).

Jane Watson Hopping

Mama's Homemade Noodles
MAKES ENOUGH FOR 8 SERVINGS

Flour as needed (some flour is dryer than others)
$^1/_2$ teaspoon salt

1 egg, slightly beaten

A little at a time, stir enough flour and salt into the beaten egg to make a very stiff dough. Roll the dough as thin as possible. Cover with a kitchen towel; do not touch for at least 30 minutes. Cut into thin strips; let them dry.

When needed, bring a large kettle of water or broth to a boil. Drop noodles into boiling liquid and cook rapidly for 15 minutes. Drain. Turn piping hot into a serving bowl.

19

Grated Celeriac, Carrot, and Apple Salad

MAKES ABOUT 6 TO 8 SERVINGS

Uncle Bud raised celeriac, which he thought added a special flavor to Aunt Sue's soups, stews, and salads. Aunty made cooked diced celeriac salads, which are crisp and flavorful, a midwinter treat when summer vegetables are not on hand.

Celeriac is a root variety of celery, about the size of a baseball and light brown in color. When used in soups and stews or cooked and chilled for use in salads, or when used raw, the skin must be removed with a vegetable peeler and the eyes must be cut out.

2 cups raw celeriac, peeled, eyes removed, grated
2 cups peeled and grated carrots
2 large apples (Golden Delicious preferred), cored but unpeeled, diced

Lettuce leaves (light green preferred)
Honey Mayonnaise (recipe follows)

In a large bowl, combine celeriac, carrots, and apples. Just before serving, arrange a bed of lettuce leaves on each of 6 to 8 medium salad plates. Spoon vegetable-and-apple mixture onto bed of lettuce. Spoon Honey Mayonnaise dressing over prepared salad.

Jane Watson Hopping

Honey Mayonnaise

1 cup mayonnaise, less if you wish
2 tablespoons honey (clover honey preferred)

Dash of grated nutmeg

In a small bowl, combine mayonnaise, honey, and nutmeg. Stir until well blended. Chill for 15 minutes before topping salad.

From *Christmas: Reflections of Winter*

In winter the northern months dance
between darkness and light
Night strides in longer boots,
sweeping blue shadows over crunching snow,
through the attic shutters of the world.

Winter is a crown of crystal and silver,
Christmas is its priceless jewel.
Radiant colors of the blazing yule
reach out, warm strangers, draw them in.
Some we once called strangers
are now our dearest friends
because of Christmas and its light.

A woodstove crackles in a timbered cottage.
A gas flame whispers blue melodies
Una vela *lights* Las Posadas
toward the laughter of las piñatas.
Candles contemplate silences
in curves of a golden bell.
The menorah remembers.

Light is heard as well as seen;
hymns from midnight churches;
from carolers a block away, clear
but distant illusions of voices,
the echoes of 20 centuries.

Christmas, the gift of light
that forever drove darkness
from the far edge of life was,
itself, announced with light.
Shepherds knelt before the star.
Wise men followed it. And found it.

Now, after centuries, the light
lives, and grows, and brightens
with every kindness
shared at Christmas
and all the days between.

May you, friend and former strangers,
walk in light forever.

—Alvin Reiss

22

Jane Watson Hopping

Reflections of Winter

When gales of wind and rain whip about the house, thunder on the roof, and beat against the windowpanes, I often stop work to build a fire on the hearth, settle in a comfortable chair, and read . . . read . . . read . . . Soon I find myself deeply engrossed in thought, reflecting on my life and the lives of others. Then I recall a bit of verse written in the early twenties by Grace E. Hall:

I ponder more and more this mystic tie
That makes us of all other life a part. . . .

When Snow Wings Fill the Air

Often in deep midwinter, Mother and all of her sisters and sisters-in-law, including Aunt Mabel, Aunt Hattie, Aunt Irene, Aunt Clary, and dear old Aunt Fanny, gathered in one kitchen or another to make batch after batch of cookies. The menfolk and older boys, and all of us children, soon tumbled in, much underfoot, and huddled in the warmth of the kitchen to bask in the heavenly fragrance of baking.

All of us were allowed to test various batches and help pack baskets that would be taken on the morrow to the sick and elderly in our community. I was probably twelve years old or older before I fully understood the thoughtfulness and generosity of these and other contributions made by the women in my family.

Along with the cookies and good wishes, Grandpa and the uncles loaded onto the wagon a little kindling and a log or more for each person they visited. The men were always sure to stay long enough to split the logs into firewood.

Jane Watson Hopping

Grandpa's Oyster Stew

MAKES ABOUT
6 SERVINGS

Each year, when oysters are in season, Grandpa has them fried or made into his favorite oyster stew. Mama would take him to town so that he could sell some of his produce or nuts and buy several pints of oysters with the money.

1 tablespoon minced onion
1 tablespoon minced celery
1 talespoon finely chopped fresh parsley
1 cup finely chopped mushrooms
2 tablespoons butter or margarine

1 1/2 cups chicken broth, homemade or store-bought
1 cup heavy cream
2 cups (1 pint) tiny drained oysters
Salt and freshly ground black pepper to taste

In a large saucepan, sauté onion, celery, parsley, and mushrooms in butter until tender but not brown. Pour chicken stock and cream into the top of a double boiler and heat until very hot but not boiling. Turn off the heat under the double boiler and add the oysters, and vegetables with their cooking butter. The hot liquid will cook the oysters, so do not heat the stew again; too much heat toughens oysters. Add salt and pepper to taste. If the stew falls below serving temperature, it can be carefully warmed. Serve in a generous soup bowl over crisp toast or with croutons or crackers.

25

Cousin Mary's Whole-Wheat Batter Bread

MAKES 1 LARGE LOAF

Our cousin Mary, who lived in Kansas, was—as Grandpa used to say—the most down-to-earth person in the world. She was loved by everyone who met her, and she told stories that brought about gales of rowdy laughter. Her cooking reflected her spirit. Cousin Mary's homemade soups were thick and well spiced, her bread wholesome and old-fashioned.

2 cups all-purpose flour
3 tablespoons sugar
1 tablespoon salt
2 tablespoons granulated yeast

1 cup milk
2 tablespoons butter or margarine
3½ cups whole-wheat flour, unsifted

In a large bowl, sift all-purpose flour with sugar and salt. Add yeast and thoroughly blend.

In a medium saucepan, combine milk, 1 cup water, and butter. Warm to lukewarm over low heat (don't bring to simmer or boil). To the all-purpose flour mixture, gradually add the warmed milk-and-water mixture. Beat by hand or with a rotary or electric mixer at medium speed for about 2 minutes, scraping the bowl with a rubber spatula occasionally. Add 1 cup of whole-wheat flour; stir into a thick batter. Add enough remaining flour to make a stiff batter; beat until well blended. Cover and let rise in a warm place until doubled in bulk, 40 to 45 minutes.

When dough is well risen, preheat oven to 375°F. Thoroughly grease a 9-by-5-by-3-inch loaf pan.

Stir the batter down and beat for a minute or two. Turn into prepared pan. Let rise again for 15 to 20 minutes. Dough should feel soft.

Bake until well risen, browned, and firm to the touch, 40 to 50 minutes. (To test for doneness, lift loaf; if it is golden brown on the bottom and turns easily out of the pan, it's done.) Remove pan from oven; leave bread

Jane Watson Hopping

in pan for 8 to 10 minutes; then, turn loaf out of pan, top side up, on a wire rack to cool. While still warm lightly grease top and sides of loaf.

Old-Fashioned Baked Apples

〜

MAKES 6 SERVINGS

In the winter, all the country people we knew had boxes and baskets of apples in the cellar or in the apple house during midwinter. The apples slaked the cold-weather desire for fresh fruits and vegetables.

6 large apples, cored (Northern Spy, Winesap, and Rome Beauty preferred)
1 to 2 tablespoons firmly packed light brown sugar for each apple

1 teaspoon butter or margarine for each apple
$1/8$ teaspoon ground cinnamon for each apple

Preheat oven to 375°F. Set out and lightly grease a large baking dish.

With a sharp knife, core and pare a 1-inch strip of peel off around the middle of the apple so that the peeling does not split (or pare peeling off the upper half of each). Place apples blossom end down in the baking dish. Fill the center of each apple with brown sugar, butter, and cinnamon. Pour water $1/4$ inch deep around apples in baking dish. If desired, spoon syrup out of the pan and spoon over apples several times during baking.

Bake until apples are tender when pierced with a fork, 30 to 40 minutes.

NOTE: Cooking time varies with size of apple.

27

For All
Its Coldest
Truths

December—why, of course we grin
And bear it—shiverin' every minute,
Yet warm from the time the month rolls in
Till it skites out with Christmas in it;
And so, for all its coldest truths
And chill, goose-pimpled imperfections,
It wads our lank old socks with Youth's
Recollections.

—From A HOOSIER CALENDAR, James Whitcomb Riley

By early December, the days have grown short and the weather stormy and cold. Country people settle down by the fire in the early darkness. By the twenty-first of the month the rays of the sun have fallen directly over the farthest point south of the equator.

Jane Watson Hopping

In polar regions the winter season lingers for half the year, in temperate zones midwinter skites through the months of December, chill January, and crocus-strewn February and into mad, rakish March. April soon brings forth thin winter sunshine, daffodils, and tulips, which brighten the landscape and lift the hearts of those who have fretted during inclement weather.

Curling

Aunt Mabel's friend Mary loved to talk about midwinter sports in Scotland, the land of her birth. Her favorite stories were about her brothers, who played in curling tournaments on the ice. Curling, a popular game in Scotland for over three hundred years, is played with large smooth stones on a rink marked out on ice.

Mary's brothers usually played on the same team. She and her sisters were their greatest fans. They shouted and waved their scarves wildly as the boys slid two stones along the ice toward a mark, or tee, thirty-eight yards distant. The object was to slide the stones closer to the mark than those of their opponents.

Ian, Mary's younger brother, was the most skilled at sweeping the ice. He and Scott worked together, under orders of Skip, their captain.

After all the stones had been thrown, or curled, from one end of the rink to the other, an inning, or end, was completed.

For Mary, her sisters Ann and Jane, and other admiring girls, the end of the game brought treats from brothers, a bit of candy, or Scotch shortbread and tea.

Jane Watson Hopping

Baked Salmon

In our area, anglers much prefer salmon caught in the ocean or at the mouths of rivers. Silver salmon are sweet-fleshed and delicious, perfect for baking. Such fish are fat enough that they need not be basted.

5-pound silver salmon, gutted, scales removed
Butter, melted
Salt and freshly ground black pepper
Sprig of parsley, left whole

2- to 3-inch piece of stalk celery, including some of the tender leaves
1/4 teaspoon dried thyme, crumbled
1 green onion, green part only, minced

Preheat oven to 350°F.

Place the whole fish on a buttered baking pan. Brush both sides slightly with melted butter. Sprinkle the cavity lightly with salt and pepper. Stuff the cavity with parsley, celery, thyme, and green onion. Cover with buttered kraft paper (a buttered brown paper bag will do).

Bake until fish flakes or until internal temperature is 140°F. Serve immediately, or cool slightly and refrigerate.

Ice Fishing

Grandpa and Uncle Ben liked to ice-fish; they chopped holes in the thick ice that lay on ponds or rivers. Sometimes they took a small homemade tent with them and set it up near the holes they had made, which gave them some shelter. Sometimes they used a hand line, a stubby rod and reel, or a tip-up device, which signaled by means of a bell or a flag when a fish was biting.

When the weather was cold and the fish quit biting, they gathered up their gear and hurried home, where they knew hot coffee and Old-Fashioned Red Bean Stew would be waiting for them.

Jane Watson Hopping

Old-Fashioned Red Bean Stew

~

MAKES 8 TO 10 SERVINGS

Aunt Mabel loved to cook. On cold wintry days she baked fragrant loaves of bread, often more than one kind. Our favorite was Herbed Creamed-Corn Corn Bread. Her father, our grandpa, bragged on the stew and corn bread while he ate several bowls of stew and consumed three or more chunks of corn bread heavily laden with fresh, light-colored, homemade butter.

1 pound seasoned pork sausage
1 yellow cooking onion, peeled and coarsely chopped
1 quart whole tomatoes
1 teaspoon salt
1 bay leaf
1/2 teaspoon freshly ground black pepper
1 1/2 teaspoons granulated garlic, or 3 small cloves garlic, minced

1 teaspoon dried thyme, crumbled
3 large or 4 medium-size red potatoes, peeled and diced
4 cups precooked red beans (canned beans can be used)
1/2 cup chopped green bell pepper
Herbed Creamed-Corn Corn Bread (recipe follows)

In a large Dutch oven, brown meat and then drain the fat off. Add onion, tomatoes, salt, bay leaf, black pepper, garlic, thyme, and diced potatoes and cook until vegetables are done, 20 minutes or more. Add red beans and simmer to blend flavors, 10 minutes. Fold chopped green pepper into hot stew. Serve immediately with Herbed Creamed-Corn Corn Bread and butter (recipe follows).

33

Herbed Creamed-Corn Corn Bread

MAKES ABOUT
12 MEDIUM SERVINGS

During the Depression era, women in our family thought this simple-to-make corn bread was a perfect bread to serve with almost any bean dish. Little they knew that corn and beans were not only a good flavor combination but a complete protein and a good substitute for meat.

1 cup all-purpose flour
1 cup yellow cornmeal
1 tablespoon baking powder
1 teaspoon salt
2 tablespoons dried basil, crumbled

2 tablespoons dried oregano, or more
2 eggs, beaten to a froth
2 cups creamed corn (one 16-ounce can)

Preheat oven to 400°F. Set out and thoroughly grease an 11-by-7-by-1½-inch baking pan.

In a large bowl, blend flour, cornmeal, baking powder, and salt. Sprinkle the herbs over the dry mixture. Pour the beaten eggs and all of the creamed-corn into a small bowl; stir to blend. Make a well in the center of the dry mixture; pour liquid mixture into the well. Stir until a soft dough is formed. Turn into the prepared baking pan. Put corn bread into the oven and bake until it is risen, light-colored on top, and golden brown on the bottom of the loaf, about 45 minutes. Serve hot or cold, with or without butter, with bean dishes, soups, or stews.

Jane Watson Hopping

Infinite designs of six-sided shapes,
They fall through winter-gray days,
or soften the night
with a blanket of sugar and diamond light.
They gather on trees, pump handles and hills
and make turbaned potentates of fence posts
and pillows of windowsills.
We see them and think they are white,
but they are seeds of colors waiting to spring
into yellow and green and rosebud and bluebird.

—SNOWFLAKES, Alvin Reiss

The Pioneer Lady's Hearty Winter Cookbook

A Pre-Christmas Singspiration

Each Christmas season, Uncle Bud and Aunt Sue invited the whole family and friends—like Ada, Ella, and Effie—to their church singspiration. Many of the friends and family members sang in the choir. Mama, who was just a little girl, thought it was a very special occasion. She still fondly recalls the holly, the cedar boughs tied with red and gold ribbons, and the tall Christmas tree strung with ropes of popped corn and hung with gilded walnuts.

Even more so, she says that she can still hear the voices of the choir and the family, who all sat close together in the front row. She mists up a bit when she tells us about Uncle Bud's rich voice that spoke so eloquently of his Savior when he sang . . .

> *Joy to the World! The Lord is come*
> *Let earth receive her King;*
> *Let every heart prepare Him room,*
> *And heaven and nature sing,*
> *And heaven and nature sing,*
> *And heaven, and heaven and nature sing.*

From JOY TO THE WORLD, Isaac Watts/George Handel

Jane Watson Hopping

Country folk in the congregation agreed that the beauty of Aunt Sue's light soprano voice singing "Silent Night" brought chills up their spines. In a small tableau, young Martha and her husband portrayed Mary and Joseph. Uncle Ned brought a lamb to church and settled it down by Mary, who took it into her lap. Little Albert had a piece to say from "Hark! The Herald Angels Sing" and his mother did not dissuade him:

> With the angelic host proclaim,
> Christ is born in Bethlehem!
> Born to raise the sons of earth;
> Born to give them second birth.
> Second Adam from above,
> Reinstate us in thy love.

When the choir had sung one ancient carol and song of praise after another, there was a sense of grace, love, and tenderness of the heart felt by everyone in the room.

The Old English Tin

(The Christmas season didn't officially begin at our home until the arrival of the old English tin.)

Grandma's Christmas Box Is Here!

Caramels twisted in waxed paper
formed the layer on the top
Followed by mittens and stocking caps
she'd knit and purled, not bought.

Black walnut fudge and divinity,
she'd neatly boxed for Dad
The caramels to his teeth would stick
and that was really bad.

In the very bottom of the tin
so carefully hidden away,
lay a tiny thin black Bible
"And don't forget to pray."

The smell of her farmhouse kitchen
lingered long inside that tin
Even in January and February
when mittens had worn thin.

—Patricia Parish Kuhn

Jane Watson Hopping

Easy-to-Make Brown Sugar Caramels

MAKES 1 POUND
OR MORE

Country women often make this candy for Christmas. Children and grown-ups alike love it. Wrapped in colorful foil and stored in an airtight container, it lasts for some time.

½ cup (1 stick) butter	1 cup light corn syrup
2 cups firmly packed brown sugar	1¾ cups light cream
¼ teaspoon salt	1 tablespoon vanilla extract

Butter lightly an 8-inch square cake pan. Melt the butter in a large saucepan, add sugar and salt; blend. Add corn syrup and stir until smooth. Add the cream gradually, stirring constantly. Cook over medium heat to a stiff-ball stage (244° to 250°F). Remove from heat and add vanilla. Pour into the pan (the candy should be about ½ to ¾ inch deep). Let cool, cut into squares, wrap, and store in an airtight container.

39

Of Strangers and Friends

Beside the big Christmas tree in the veterans' home
Old Army studies the Zippo he's carried since Bastogne.
He thumbs it to flame, and after a puff,
gruffly, but gently, says,
"Get on with the game"
to the kid who made him the chessmen.
Once a stranger, the kid's his friend.
They've spent a lot of holidays together.
Outside, the weather is brittle and white.
Lights from the tree color the snow on the sill.
Old Army remembers The Bulge and '44
and that Christmas when Gen. McAuliffe,
bless his airborne brass, answered
the enemy's order to surrender with "Nuts."
The kid's got class, Army thinks.
Glancing from a wreath of smoke,
once again to colors on crusted snow,
he thinks, again, that they are brothers.
Brother? He could be the kid's dad.
He is old enough, he knows, and he knows
the kid paid different dues, in a rice paddy.
Across the room men and women,
survivors of a different war,
brothers and sisters of different faiths
join their voices to sing songs of peace
and good will. Defenders of the light.
Tree lights scatter colors on the snow.
Old Army says again, "Get on with the game,"
and softly "Merry Christmas, my friend."

—From CHRISTMAS: REFLECTIONS OF WINTER, Alvin Reiss

Old Army

Jane Watson Hopping

Songs of Peace

Who better can sing the songs of peace than those who

have sung the songs of war? In the depth of their souls,

do they know more about peace than any of us? In their

dreams, do they hear voices that say:

> *If there is righteousness in the heart,*
> *Will there be beauty in one's character?*
> *If there is beauty in character*
> *Will there be harmony in the home?*
> *If there is harmony in the home*
> *Will there be order in the nation?*
> *If there is order in the nation,*
> *Will there be peace in the world?*

—PEACE, Author Unknown

Over There

When Uncle Edward came home from "The War to End All Wars," his mental and physical health was none too good. He had no blood relatives to take him in. So Aunt Clary told him, "Come and stay with me for a while." She fed him and made him feel at home in her comfortable back bedroom.

When he got stronger, he told her how much he appreciated her kindness. One day he packed up his things and asked Floyd to take him over to the Veterans' Home, where he lived out the rest of his life—"among friends," as he put it.

Jane Watson Hopping

One-Dish Dinner

This easy-to-make dish is similar to one that Uncle Arch jotted down and brought home in his pocket from France in 1917. The women in our family took to it, in part because it could be made ahead of time, refrigerated, taken out shortly before supper, and cooked with other dishes.

1 pound lean ground chuck
1 medium-size to large onion, peeled and sliced, as desired
1 tablespoon oil or fat, or more, as needed
Salt and freshly ground black pepper to taste

4 medium potatoes, peeled and sliced
1/2 teaspoon Worcestershire sauce
4 cups canned whole tomatoes, with juice
Diced green bell pepper and celery (optional)

Preheat oven to 350°F. Set out a medium skillet and a lightly buttered 2-quart casserole dish.

Brown meat and onion in skillet; add a tablespoon of oil or fat. Salt and pepper lightly. Arrange potatoes in the bottom of a 2-quart casserole dish. Spoon meat and onion over top of potatoes. Add Worcestershire to tomatoes; pour over all. Sprinkle with diced green pepper and celery as you wish.

Bake until vegetables are fork-tender, about 1 1/2 hours. Serve while piping hot with heated rolls.

The Holy Night, from the painting by Corregio

Jane Watson Hopping

From *Christmas: The Time of the Child*

The road lay a dream behind her,
a long and winding memory
of looking ahead, past dust, past tired
ears of a donkey led
by rough and gentle hands
of the carpenter who had chosen her.

Deep in the winter of our northern world
we celebrate the renewal of life,
the gift of the Child.

As she rode, she felt the life that moved
within her,
in that moment still hers alone,
the child of no man;
the child of infinite
grace and love;
the child of this woman
so lately a child herself.
On the road the child
was not yet of this world,
but one with her.
She dreamed, and smiled.

Christmas is the time of the child.

Now the child lives in her arms,
radiant, silent, sleeping.
She holds her son against her breast,
feels his warmth against her heart.
Closing her eyes, she dreams.

Softly touched by the carpenter's hand,
she wakens to kneeling shepherds.
Her heart sings,
and the heavens.

Come to the stable on wings of the heart
and kneel.
Christmas is the gift of eternal tomorrows.

Christmas is the gift of the Child.

—Alvin Reiss

Come to the Stable on Wings of the Heart

Aunt Fanny loves to recall one particular church pageant of her youth. She was only eight or ten years old when she played the role of the Virgin Mary. The pageant took place in a rough shed built by her uncle and father. Behind the shed, Joseph, played by her cousin Michael, had gathered about himself the beasts of the field, several black sheep and two or three white ones, and a borrowed donkey.

Coal oil lamps lit the scene. The first faint signs of dawn tinged the hills and sky painted on a large white flannel sheet that was the backdrop for the pageant. Bathed in light and wrapped in swaddling cloth, the Johnsons' baby boy was held by Mary. He looked every bit like the baby of old, who was said to have

Aunt Fanny and Uncle John

Jane Watson Hopping

shone with a heavenly radiance. Mary, kneeling before a manger filled with straw, laid the babe to rest. An old shepherd looked at them in amazement, raising his hand to his head as if afraid that it was all a dream. Behind the crèche, angels stood amidst billowing clouds made of quilt batting and gazed upon the scene, reflecting on the Christ Child's birth.

> *God bless your Christmas wherever you are*
> *And keep your courage bright;*
> *For the spirit of man is the candle of God,*
> *And it burns on the darkest night.*

—GOD BLESS YOUR CHRISTMAS!, Hazel Adams

In the Arms of Memory

Aunt Clary's favorite Christmas was in 1908. She was nine years old that year, and already an excellent reader, a lover of fairy tales and stories about Santa Claus and the Easter Bunny.

By the third week of December, she was begging to set up the Christmas tree, going through the family recipes for holiday cookie recipes, talking incessantly about Santa Claus, and making homemade gifts for everyone, even her brother Joseph.

On Christmas Eve, she sang carols for the family and caroled with neighborhood children. Then she crawled into her soft featherbed, covered herself with a downy comforter, put out the coal oil lamp, and worried that she would not be able to stay awake until Santa Claus came down the chimney.

As she drifted off to sleep, she thought she heard the tramping of little feet on the rooftop. This was followed by a noise in the chimney; a rubbing, scratching, bumping; and then suddenly a clattering thump in the fireplace.

Aunty sat up in bed. She could see an old man stuffing mysterious packages into her stocking and putting beribboned packages on the mantelpiece.

The Jolly Old Elf looked about the room for a minute. "Poor little girl," he said to himself. "She will not have any presents! She saw me; she has broken the rules." With that, he left.

Aunt Clary began to cry. She called out to Santa, "Dear Santa, come back and forgive me. I meant no harm. Come back! Come back!" Then she fell back on her pillow and cried all the more.

When she saw that Santa's bag was getting light, she stopped crying and lay quietly until she was asleep. After a while, she felt someone kissing her. She opened her eyes. It was daylight, and her mama was bending over her. "Merry Christmas, Clary," her mother said to her. When she saw that her child had been crying, she said, "What is it, dear? Today is Christmas Day!"

"I dreamed that because I laid awake to watch for Santa Claus, he didn't leave me anything!"

Her mother kissed her and held her for a while. Then she said, "Clary, dear, that was only a dream. Look at the mantelpiece, the Christmas tree, and your stocking."

"He didn't forget me!" Clary exclaimed. Aunty then told anyone who would listen about her dream. Old Uncle Bill told her that Santa Claus loved children and that he would never deliberately spoil a child's Christmas.

Jane Watson Hopping

A Simple Country Eggnog

MAKES 2 TO 3 CUPS

Mother always milked two cows, and so she always had an abundance of milk and cream. She sold it and shared it liberally with her sisters and friends. When we were children, she made this drink for us and often served it at midwinter parties and get-togethers.

2 eggs, separated
2 tablespoons sugar
Pinch of salt
2 cups milk

Pinch of ground cinnamon
Pinch of grated nutmeg
Whipped cream (optional)

In a medium bowl, beat egg yolks; add sugar, salt, and milk, and stir in until blended. Beat the egg whites until stiff and add them, with the cinnamon and nutmeg. Sometimes she added whipped cream to make a richer drink.

December

*The soul of music lingers
When the sound has died away;
The twilight lays cool fingers
On the throbbing pulse of day;
The love we best remember
Bears the blur of hottest tears,
And the snows of late December
Are the ashes of our years.*

—Grace E. Hall, *Patchwork*

Lingering Thoughts of December

God's love to all mankind
is wrapped and sealed
in one glorious word
Peace!

—From PEACE, Grace Noll Crowell

As December wanes, I find myself caught up in the flood of days that pass by me. The Christmas season flashes by, as does the onset of a new year. All about me mountain peaks are covered with snow. Hanging in our fingerling valleys is a soft mist full of the promise of rain.

Nights are cold and frosty. The cattle are protected from them with their heavy coats of deep red hair. The calves, well fed on mother's milk and abundant winter grasses, are growing fast.

The children are still playing Christmas and don't want the tree taken down. Hannah, who had a birthday on the twenty-third of December, is still centered in the middle of the floor with treasures piled high around her. Rachel, who was Mary, mother of Jesus, in her church pageant, still dons her robes and reads to the little ones about Jesus, who was born in Bethlehem.

Jane Watson Hopping

Christmas Stars

MAKES 6 TO 8 DOZEN COOKIES

Aunt Irene generally hosted a pre-Christmas party for the family. All of the aunties brought cookies. Grown-ups and children alike sang songs. Uncle Ben led the mittened and scarfed family to nearby houses to sing carols to older folk. We children went up on the porches, knocked on the doors, and wished them all a Merry Christmas.

1 cup (2 sticks) butter or margarine, softened at room temperature
1½ cups sugar
3 eggs
1 teaspoon vanilla extract

3½ cups all-purpose flour
2 teaspoons cream of tartar
1 teaspoon baking soda
½ teaspoon salt
Ornamental Frosting (recipe follows)

Preheat oven to 375°F. Set out a large baking sheet or two smaller ones.

In a large bowl, cream butter; add sugar and beat until light and fluffy. Add eggs one at a time, beating after each addition. Blend in vanilla. Into a medium bowl, sift flour with cream of tartar, baking soda, and salt. Stir flour mixture into creamed mixture. Cover and chill for 3 hours or more.

When thoroughly chilled, remove the dough from refrigerator. Turn onto a well-floured surface. Roll dough to ¼-inch thickness. Cut into large or small star shapes, as desired. Place on baking sheets, ½ inch apart.

Bake until cookies are risen, lightly browned around the edges, and firm to the touch, 6 to 8 minutes. Let cool on baking sheets for 5 minutes; let finish cooling on wire rack. Meanwhile, prepare Ornamental Frosting. Spread lightly over stars.

Ornamental Frosting

¹/₄ cup (¹/₂ stick) butter or margarine,
    softened at room temperature
4 cups powdered sugar, sifted
2 egg whites, unbeaten

1 teaspoon vanilla extract
¹/₄ teaspoon cream of tartar
1 to 2 teaspoons light cream

In a medium bowl, cut butter or margarine into powdered sugar until the mixture has the texture of uncooked rice. Then add egg whites, vanilla, and cream of tartar. Beat thoroughly. Blend in cream and continue beating until frosting is of a spreading consistency.

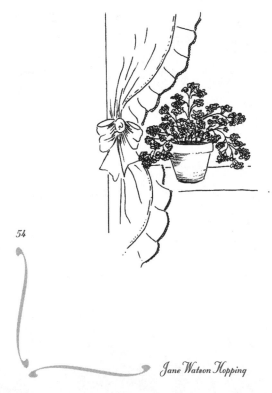

Jane Watson Hopping

Winter in the Sierras

The pines are black on Sierra's slope,
And white are the drifted snows;
The flowers are gone, the buckthorn bare,
And chilly the north wind blows.
The pine-boughs creak,
And the pine-trees speak
A language the north wind knows.

There's never a track leads in or out
Of the cave of the big brown bear;
The squirrels have hid in their deepest holes,
And fastened the doors with care.
The red fox prowls,
And the lean wolf howls
As he hunts far down from the lair.

The eagle hangs on the wing all day,
On the chance of a single kill;
The little gray hawk hunts far and wide
Before he can get his fill.
The snow-wreaths sift,
And the blown snows drift
To the canyons deep and still.

—Mary Austin

Brittle, White Weather

When snow falls through the night, blanketing the farm with icy snow crystals, I call the children to come and see the moonlight shining on the snow. We put our winter gear on and shuffle our way to the barn and back, all the while listening to the snow crunch beneath our feet.

How long can this last? Through late December? From New Year's Day until spring?

In the morning, a flock of children drop by to play in the fields. After they have played in the crisp air all morning, knowing that my fire is burning, sending wafts of warmth throughout the house, they come knocking at my door. It's time for hot chocolate. By late afternoon we see soft-feathered snowflakes begin to fall again. The whole earth knows that

"In Deepest Winter" by Cameron Squires, age 12. (Silver badge.)

Jane Watson Hopping

December is on the wane. Spring, dressed in sunbeams, beckons with a pastel hand to travel with her from the time of want to the time of plenty.

New Year's Eve Vigil

Dear Father-God, I thank Thee gratefully
For this new year, filled full with precious days
Wherein I may serve Thee with heart and hand
And speak Thy word of love in helpful ways.

—From PRAYER FOR A NEW YEAR, Gordon Frantz

New Year's Eve celebrations are of two kinds: the prayer or watch meetings of the church, and the pandemonium of carnival or of the sportive sort. Each of these customs has been handed down for generations.

Mama has vivid memories of New Year's Eve watch meetings in the Southern Baptist church of her childhood. Her father played the mandolin and sang favorite old hymns, along with his many sisters who sang with the choir. The church was candlelit, and the murmured prayers wafted through the room. Some folk took the opportunity to testify about God's gifts to them, others spoke of healing that saved their children from the ravishing

illnesses of the day. Many offered prayers of thankfulness.

Even today Mama sings Grandpa's favorite hymns:

> *He leadeth me! O blessed tho't!*
> *O words with heav'nly comfort fraught!*
> *What-e'er I do, whe-e-er I be,*
> *Still 'tis God's hand that leadeth me.*
>
> *He leadeth me, He leadeth me,*
> *By His own hand He leadeth me;*
> *His faithful foll'wer I would be,*
> *For by His hand He leadeth me.*
>
> —From HE LEADETH ME, J. H. Gilmore/Wm. B. Bradbury

After the choir sang, the congregation sang favorite hymns like "Hidden

Peace," written by John S. Brown and L. O. Brown, which comforted the

hard-pressed and lonely:

> *I cannot tell thee whence it came,*
> *This peace within my breast;*
> *But this I know, there fills my soul*
> *A strange and tranquil rest.*
>
> *Beneath the toil and care of life,*
> *This hidden stream flows on;*
> *My weary soul no longer thirsts,*
> *Nor am I sad and alone.*

Jane Watson Hopping

Mama still talks about a woman preacher whose gentle ways encouraged her flock to find grace in life. She talked to children about kindness and the importance of school in their lives, and about parents who sacrificed many things in order to create a good life for them.

The congregation in her church was made up of families all sitting together: grandparents, parents, young people, and little children. Mama recalls singing with the children's choir:

> When He cometh, when He cometh,
> To make up His jewels,
> All his jewels precious jewels
> His loved and His own,
> He will gather. He will gather
> the gems for His kingdom,
> All the pure ones, all the bright ones,
> His loved and His own
>
> Like the stars of the morning,
> His bright crown adorning.

—From JEWELS, Rev. Wm. O. Cushing/George F. Root

59

Old-Fashioned Chess Pie

Grandpa liked sweet cakes, dried fruit, and syrup pies like pecan pie or this old-time Chess Pie. Mother loved to make apple pies, pear pies, and, of course, pumpkin pies to take to the New Year's Vigil. She made a pair of these sweet walnut pies, one for her father, and one for sharing with other old men in the congregation.

Butter-Crust Pastry (recipe follows)
3 large eggs, lightly beaten
1 cup sugar
2 tablespoons all-purpose flour
1 cup light corn syrup (dark may be substituted)

2 tablespoons butter or margarine, melted
1 teaspoon vanilla extract
1 1/2 cups coarsely chopped walnuts

Preheat oven to 400°F. Make pastry before preparing filling. Line a 9-inch pie pan with pastry, leaving a 1-inch overlap. Turn overlapping dough under and flute edge of dough.

In a medium bowl, combine eggs, sugar, flour, corn syrup, butter, and vanilla; blend well. Pour into unbaked, prepared pie shell. Spread walnuts over top. Bake in lower third of oven until pastry is risen and firmed up, about 15 minutes. Reduce temperature to 350°F and bake until the center appears set, 35 to 45 minutes more (total baking time 50 to 60 minutes). Transfer to a wire rack and let cool thoroughly.

Butter-Crust Pastry MAKES ONE 9-INCH PASTRY SHELL

1 cup all-purpose flour, plus flour for rolling out dough
1/2 teaspoon salt

1/2 cup (1 stick) cold butter

Jane Watson Hopping

In a large bowl sift flour with salt. Cut the butter in, using 2 pastry knives, a pastry blender, or your fingertips until all of the dough particles are the size of small peas. Gradually sprinkle water over the dough, using just enough to moisten. At the same time, stir with a fork until particles have gathered into a loose dough. Turn out onto a floured, flat surface and shape into a ball. Chill if you wish for later use or roll out freshly made dough and line pie pan.

Hot Apple Cider Punch

MAKES ABOUT 16 CUPS

Our old families made their own cider and often served it when folks came to visit or when a hot drink was needed for a New Year's Vigil at the church.

1 gallon apple cider	$^2/_3$ cup hot water
6–8 whole cloves	Sugar to taste
2 teaspoons whole allspice	2 oranges studded with cloves
2 three-inch cinnamon sticks	

In a large soup kettle or saucepan, heat cider, cloves, allspice, cinnamon, hot water, and sugar to boiling. Cover and simmer for about 20 minutes. Strain the punch, then turn into a heatproof bowl. Float studded oranges in the punch.

61

Ties with the Past

Mama still tells stories about her childhood. She lived deep in Missouri farm country. Her favorite story is about Christmas, deep snow, and a New Year's Vigil at the old Baptist church. Throughout these stories, Mama tells how nearby country roads disappeared amid the icy, frosted countryside.

She often reminisces about friends, family, and neighbors who braved the weather to settle down by the fire of her mother's kitchen cookstove, swaddled in handmade quilts or home-woven wool blankets. Some brought leftover holiday cookies to eat with steaming hot coffee and tea. Others, like Hannah and Floyd, brought meat or vegetable dishes for the noonday meal.

Mother recalls playing games and eating goodies with the other children. She most loved the warm corners of the house that hosted little girls who told each other delightful secrets.

By midday, some of the men had decided to ride their horses through the woods into town. Women visited and waited, knowing that their menfolk would be talking with merchants, buyers, and others about winter wheat, cattle, well-bred bulls, and spring feeder lambs. The women talked about laying hens and being able to sell young fryers to the townfolk. They glowed, anticipating the pleasure again of having egg money of their own.

In the late afternoon, when early winter darkness began to fall, women began to gather up coats, scarves, and baskets of goodies.

The men who rode back from town were in a hurry to bundle everyone up and head home. "It's gettin' late," they would tell their wives. The men would help settle the children in the wagons and make sure that all were warmly wrapped in blankets.

A new year had come! New plans were afoot! Friendships had been rekindled! As every one called out their good-byes and children clung to the hands of their friends and cousins, the women hugged and said to one another, "You have filled my well of loneliness!" This was answered with, "When the weather breaks we'll come over to see you!"

Floyd's Favorite Pot Roast

MAKES 6 TO 8
SERVINGS

Floyd's wife, Hannah, often invited Aunt Clary and Uncle John to come for supper. One of her favorite meals was pot roast with carrots and potatoes, served with a side-dish of sautéed kohlrabi and Simple Hot Rolls (page 107).

4 pounds beef (round, chuck, or heel)	1 teaspoon dried thyme, crumbled
1/2 cup flour	1/4 cup meat drippings or margarine
1 teaspoon salt	4 or 5 small onions
1/2 teaspoon pepper	6 small to medium-size carrots
	4 or 5 large potatoes

Set out a large Dutch oven.

Tie meat with a strong cord to keep it in place, or ask the butcher to do it. In a small platter, combine flour, salt, pepper, and thyme. Wipe the meat with a clean, damp kitchen cloth. Then thoroughly coat meat with flour mixture. Heat the fat in the Dutch oven; when hot, brown meat on all sides. Add 1 cup water. Cover and simmer gently for 3 to 4 hours. Turn meat occasionally. Add more water if needed.

Meanwhile, peel the onions and carrots, and peel and quarter the potatoes. An hour before pot roast is done, add onions, carrots, and potatoes. When meat is tender and vegetables done, remove pot roast and vegetables from hot pan. Cover with another pan to keep warm. When ready to serve, transfer meat to a platter and arrange vegetables around it. Make brown gravy.

Brown Gravy

Remove liquid from pan and skim off fat. For each cup of gravy needed, measure out 1 cup liquid. In a small to medium-size saucepan, heat 2 tablespoons fat for each cup of liquid; stir in 2 tablespoons flour for each cup of liquid and cook together to make a roux. Add liquid and blend well until gravy has a rich brown color. Stir constantly. Blend in 1 cup cold water. Season with salt and pepper. Return to heat and cook until thickened, 3 to 5 minutes.

Hannah's Sautéed Kohlrabi

MAKES 6 OR MORE SERVINGS

Aunt Clary's friend Hannah still clung to old-country ways; she spoke fluent German and English, depending on who she was talking to. She loved to cook for company and would make old-country dishes to please her guests. While she cooked, she liked to share old-world vocabulary. She told Aunt Clary that *Kohl* in German meant "cabbage," and *Rabi* meant "turnip." She was generous with her recipes, sharing them freely with other women.

6 or more kohlrabi
1/4 cup butter, melted
Salt and freshly ground black pepper

1 cup beef broth, homemade or store-bought
1 pint sour cream

Discard leaves of kohlrabi and wash and peel it. Cut into small finger-size pieces and sauté in a heavy-bottomed skillet in hot butter, over low heat, without browning. Season with salt and pepper. Add broth, 1 tablespoon at a time, shaking the pan at intervals so the pieces don't stick to the bottom. Continue steaming over low heat until tender. Add enough sour cream to make a sauce. Continue to heat but do not boil. Serve with pot roast and Simple Hot Rolls (page 107).

65

Date-Filled Oatmeal-Nut Bars

~

MAKES ABOUT 42
2-BY-2-INCH BARS

One midwinter day, when rain poured down over the farm, Colleen and I decided to make up a recipe for these wholesome cookies. There was one thing wrong with them, they just wouldn't keep—by next morning busy fingers had been grabbing them and greedy mouths had been testing them. Everyone decided that they were delicious, a real treat with milk, tea, or boiling hot coffee.

3 cups dates (commercially prepared for baking)
1 1/2 cups hot water
3/4 cup (1 1/2 sticks) margarine
3/4 cup firmly packed light brown sugar
2 jumbo eggs, beaten to a froth
2 cups all-purpose flour

1 1/2 teaspoons baking powder
1 teaspoon salt
1 teaspoon ground cinnamon, plus 1 teaspoon more for topping
1/2 teaspoon grated nutmeg
4 cups quick-cooking oatmeal
1/2 cup sunflower seeds, plus 1/2 cup more for topping

Preheat oven to 400°F. Thoroughly grease and set aside an 11 1/2-by-17 1/2-by-1-inch jelly roll pan.

In a medium saucepan, reconstitute dates by adding 1 1/2 cups hot water. Stir until blended. Place date-water mixture over medium heat; stir until thick filling is formed. Set aside to cool.

In a large bowl, combine margarine, brown sugar, and eggs and beat until well blended. Into a medium bowl, sift flour with baking powder, salt, 1 teaspoon cinnamon, and nutmeg. Stir flour mixture into liquid ingredients; add 2 cups of the oatmeal and blend well. Stir in remaining oatmeal, a little at a time, and blend with fingertips until crumbly. Fold in 1/2 cup sunflower seeds. Press two-thirds of the dough into bottom of the prepared pan. Spread cooled filling over dough; pat remaining dough over filling. Sprinkle with remaining 1/2 cup sunflower seeds and dust with cinnamon.

Jane Watson Hopping

Bake until bars are slightly risen, light brown, and soft to the touch, about 18 minutes. Remove from oven and set pan on wire rack to cool. Cut into bars when lukewarm or cold.

NOTE: When placed in airtight freezer bag and frozen, bars stay fresh for two or more months.

When the Cold Gets Stronger

The month of January is the coldest time of year. Old-timers say, "When the days get longer, the cold gets stronger." Thick ice settles on ponds, filligreed fences decorate the landscape, broken water pipes spew freezing water into the air. Delighted country and city folk, heavily mittened and scarved, brave the brittle, white weather to look at nature's display.

Lingering Memories of Midwinter Feasts

The midwinter thaw brought melting snow and ice. Heavy rains washed through the countryside, creeks rose to capacity, and water raced across country roads and through small towns. Grandpa and Grandma's neighbors would come for miles to check on friends and relatives. Sometimes menfolk hitched up buggies and farm wagons and drove out into the countryside to gather up cousins who were struggling through a time of want and old folks who were not strong enough to stand against the weather alone.

Jane Watson Hopping

Grandpa took some of the older children with him and drove out to Aunt Clary's house and then to Floyd and Hannah's. On the way there, he told all of the children they should always remember to look out for old folks, to make sure they were swaddled in warm blankets of their own or blankets Grandma had sent along with him for them.

He told Aunt Clary and Floyd and Hannah not to bring anything except each other. Uncle Fred, who was about four or five years old, kissed Aunt Clary and said, "Don't worry, old Aunty! We got cookies and good vittles everywhere!"

Stuffed Flank Steak Baked in Buttermilk

MAKES 6 SERVINGS

Our mother always tenderized beef with buttermilk. Effie, who loved new recipes, brought this one to Mother's house while we still lived in Missouri. It has been a family favorite for at least sixty years.

$2^{1}/_{2}$ cups soft whole-wheat bread crumbs
$^{1}/_{3}$ cup butter or margarine, melted
1 tablespoon chopped onion
1 teaspoon salt

Dash of pepper
1 flank steak, $1^{1}/_{2}$ to 2 pounds
2 cups buttermilk
$^{1}/_{4}$ cup flour

Preheat oven to 350°F. Set out a large, covered baking dish.

To make stuffing, mix bread crumbs, butter, onion, $^{1}/_{2}$ teaspoon of the salt, and the pepper together in a medium bowl. Lay steak out flat; spread filling over the steak, roll up, tuck in ends, and tie with a string or fasten with skewers. Sprinkle the remaining salt over the top.

In a small amount of butter, brown rolled steak on all sides; place in baking dish. Pour the buttermilk over the stuffed roll, cover, and bake until meat is tender, about $1^{1}/_{2}$ hours.

Remove roll from pan; transfer to a deep platter; keep warm. Pour remaining pan drippings from the baking dish into a deep saucepan; beat with rotary beater, then strain. Add flour, mixed to a paste with a little water, and cook, stirring constantly, until sauce is thick. Pour over meat.

Jane Watson Hopping

Golden Glow Broccoli

After our family moved to California, Aunt Irene introduced us to broccoli. It took a while for us to decide that we liked this member of the cole family. One particular event won us over: she invited us all to her house for dinner. She served a delicious pot roast with potatoes, onions, and carrots, which pleased Uncle Arch and Grandpa. And she set out a large flat serving dish of Golden Glow Broccoli, which we all savored with pleasure.

1½ pounds fresh broccoli
1 cup mayonnaise
Juice of 1 lemon
1 teaspoon grated onion

¼ teaspoon dried basil, crumbled
6 hard-cooked egg yolks, sieved
(finely chop and reserve egg whites)
1 cup diced mushrooms

In a large saucepan, cook broccoli in a modest amount of boiling salted water until just tender. Drain and set aside.

In a small saucepan, thoroughly combine and heat mayonnaise, lemon juice, onion, and basil. Turn broccoli into a serving dish. Pour warm dressing over broccoli and sprinkle with sieved egg yolks.

Make 2 cups Medium White Sauce (recipe follows). Add egg whites and mushrooms and spoon over buttered toast.

71

Medium White Sauce   MAKES 2 CUPS

This sauce, used for creamed or scalloped foods, has the consistency of cream.

¹/₄ cup (¹/₂ stick) butter or margarine
¹/₄ cup all-purpose flour
¹/₂ teaspoon salt

¹/₄ teaspoon freshly ground pepper (white preferred)
2 cups milk (2% preferred)

Over low heat, melt the butter. Blend in the flour, salt, and pepper. Cook, stirring, until the mixture is smooth and bubbling. Remove from heat. Stir milk into butter-flour mixture. Return to heat. Stir constantly until sauce is boiling, then stir 1 minute more to thicken. Remove from heat.

A Favorite Midwinter Dessert

∽

MAKES 4 SERVINGS

Every summer Mother canned a hundred quarts of free-stone and cling peaches for winter. All through the frozen months, we ate them plain and in pies, in cobblers, and in other simple desserts like this one.

8 canned peach halves (cling peaches preferred)
¹/₃ cup raspberry jelly

1 pint vanilla ice cream (store-bought preferred)

Jane Watson Hopping

Set out 4 dessert dishes.

Place 2 peach halves in each dish. In a small saucepan, melt jelly over low heat; pour over peach halves. Chill for 2 or 3 hours. Just before serving, top each plate with a scoop of vanilla ice cream.

Ada's Spiced Tea

MAKES 4 CUPS OR MORE

On wintry days, when the ladies came to visit, Ada made her special spiced tea. The women talked about children and made plans for helping those who were "having a hard time of it." Two or three of them brought a plate of cookies with them. Some agreed to take Aunt Clary and Floyd a generous pot of soup. Others lent a hand to families who were broke by helping them make bread. Old Aunt Fanny told them all, "Bread has always been the staff of life."

4 teaspoons loose tea (Earl Grey preferred)
6 cloves, whole or crushed
$1/2$ teaspoon grated orange zest

$1/4$ cup orange juice
$1/2$ teaspoon ground cinnamon
$1/4$ teaspoon grated nutmeg
4 cups boiling water

Place tea, cloves, orange zest, cinnamon, and nutmeg in a heatproof container and pour boiling water over them. Cover and let steep for 3 to 5 minutes. Stir and strain. Serve piping hot.

Cold and Lovely Month

Aunt Mae grew up in New England. At ninety-six years of age she could still remember wonderful stories about her childhood. One of our favorites was of harvesting ice in January, when she would be allowed to go with her father to the river, where deep layers of ice were being cut. Her mother would bundle her up and tell her to "stand back and just watch, and to mind Papa."

She vividly recalled harvesters scraping the ice clean of dirt and snow. Sometimes her stories faltered, for she had difficulty describing the monstrous machinery of her childhood. She would talk with wonder about the flowing river of summer, and with amazement about the marker that cut a series of grooves about three feet apart up and down the ice-choked river, and then cut crosswise through the ice, making parallel grooves that defined each block of ice.

When her father stopped work to pour himself a cup of black tea, he showed her a plow that was also a marker of ice. It was fitted with a steel bar, which in turn was fitted with sharp knives that followed along behind the

marker. "Mae," he told her, pointing at a power saw, "stay back from the river's edge, and I'll come back and pour a cup of hot tea for you and sweeten it with honey and cool it with milk."

So she waited patiently, watching and listening to the power saw, which had a rotating wheel with a sawtooth edge. Once the cakes of ice were pulled loose from the great sheets of ice, they were floated ashore through channels in the ice. Then they were hauled out of the water, dragged to the icehouse in town, and packed in sawdust.

That June or July, her father took her to the icehouse and showed her how the walls were insulated with sawdust. She sat on a burlap bag and one of the men's coats on a large block of ice. Finally, her father lifted her off and rubbed her hands and feet and asked if she was too cold. Her father then paid a man named Jake to deliver ice regularly to their house. Fifty pounds would just fit in the icebox.

Aunt Mae could recall stories about her great-grandfather, who sailed on a clipper ship from New York City to Charleston, South Carolina, with a cargo of natural blocks of ice around the year 1800. At that time there was quite an ice trade between the Northern and Southern states. By the 1880s, clipper ships carried blocks of ice to many parts of the world, not only to our own Southern ports but also to the Western gold fields of California, and other countries, like the West Indies and India.

When Skaters and Crystals Dance

Gliding gracefully across the frozen pond
Etching perfect figure eights skaters and crystals dance
In the moonlight until the hour is late.

—PERFECT FIGURE EIGHTS, Patricia Parish Kuhn

Jane Watson Hopping

Children living near Ada's house flew through figure eights on frozen ponds, leaving a trail of ice crystals. Some dipped and swirled like dancers; others, mainly boys, raced around the ponds and bet on who would be the first around. A loser might have to give up his best pocket knife or a marble collection.

Girls tended to be more graceful. They danced over the ice, curls flying in the breeze, each hoping that young Ted Brown, whose father was the town doctor, would ask them to skate with him.

Ada recalls going down to the pond to watch the newest generation of skaters, only to reminisce fondly about the day Albert, now her husband, had asked her to skate with him. He was about nineteen and splendid—a strong, skillful skater who was not only graceful but powerful enough to win almonst every race on every pond.

And as Albert told his competitors, he ended up with the best prize of all: sixteen-year-old Ada!

Baby Lima Bean Soup

MAKES 8 OR MORE
SERVINGS

On cold wintry days, Aunt Fanny would put on a pot of beans, then call and invite all of the family to supper. When the younger women asked her what she would like to have them bring, she would ask for Aunt Mabel's California Cole Slaw (page 79), Mother's Herbed Northern Corn Bread (page 80), and Aunt Irene's Winter Apple Pie with Cheddar Cheese (page 81). Other aunties and family friends would bring whatever they wished.

$1^1/_2$ cups dry baby lima beans
  7 cups hot water
    About a pound of ham, or a ham bone with about a pound of meat clinging to it
  1 small winter cooking onion, peeled and chopped

  2 stalks celery, chopped fine
  1 teaspoon salt
$^1/_4$ teaspoon freshly ground black pepper

Put beans in a large soup pot; add the 7 cups hot water. Over high heat, boil beans for 2 minutes. Remove from heat. Let soak for 1 hour—or overnight, if preferred.

Add ham to soup pot with onion, celery, salt, and pepper. Simmer, covered, until beans are soft, about 2 hours or more. When done, remove ham or ham bone from beans and put on a platter. Cube piece of ham or trim meat off bone and cube. Set aside. While still hot, mash beans. Turn cubes of ham into the soup.

NOTE: When tripled, this recipe makes 18 to 24 servings.

Jane Watson Hopping

Aunt Mabel's California Cole Slaw

MAKES 6 TO 8 SERVINGS

Aunt Mabel, Uncle Arch, and Uncle Ben and their marriage partners lived in the foothills of the California mountains for several years before Grandpa, Aunt Hattie, the cousins, Mother, Daddy, and I settled there. We loved the hilly country, with its orchards and vineyards. Of course, we all loved most that the family was close together again.

1 small head of green cabbage, trimmed (Golden Acre preferred)
2 tart apples, cored, peeled, and chopped
1 small sweet red onion, peeled and minced
1 2-ounce jar pimientos, minced
1 cup celery (tender white center stalks), trimmed and finely chopped
1 tablespoon honey
1 teaspoon dry mustard
1/4 teaspoon salt
1 cup sour cream
Minced fresh parsley

Into a medium-large bowl, shred trimmed cabbage. Add apples, onion, pimientos, and celery. In a medium bowl, stir together honey, dry mustard, and salt. Mix thoroughly. Blend sour cream into honey mixture. Turn dressing onto salad vegetables and toss. Sprinkle minced parsley in and on top of salad.

Mother's Herbed Northern Corn Bread

MAKES 9 TO 12 SERVINGS

Mama and Grandpa loved corn bread, so along with buttermilk biscuits she often served herbed corn bread with Aunt Fanny's Baby Lima Bean Soup.

1 cup yellow cornmeal (white, if preferred)
1 cup all-purpose flour
2 tablespoons sugar
4 teaspoons baking powder
1/2 teaspoon salt

1 teaspoon dried parsley, crumbled
1 teaspoon dried thyme, crumbled
1 cup milk
1/4 cup (1/2 stick) butter or margarine, softened at room temperature
1 egg, beaten to a froth

Preheat oven to 425°F. Set out and thoroughly grease a 9-by-9-by-2-inch baking pan.

In a medium to large bowl, blend cornmeal, flour, sugar, baking powder, salt, parsley, and thyme. In a small bowl, combine milk, softened butter, and egg.

Make a well in the cornmeal mixture. Pour the milk-egg mixture into the well and, using a fork, stir it into the cornmeal mixture, stirring just enough to moisten the batter.

Pour into prepared pan. Bake until risen, golden brown on bottom and sides of loaf, and firm to the touch. Remove from oven and set on wire rack to cool. While still hot, turn out upside down onto a plate or platter. Cut into squares.

Jane Watson Hopping

Aunt Irene's Winter Apple Pie with Cheddar Cheese

MAKES ONE 9-INCH PIE

Aunty loved to bake! Her pastry was not only good to eat but also well put together. Her crusts were light brown and crisp, the edges fluted to perfection. We little cousins all loved to be invited to her house for supper along with our parents. We knew that she would have made special treats just for us.

Pastry for Two-Crust Pie (recipe follows)
3/4 cup sugar
1/2 cup all-purpose flour
1/2 teaspoon ground cinnamon
1/4 teaspoon grated nutmeg
Dash of salt

6 cups pared and thinly sliced tart apples (Winesaps preferred)
2 tablespoons butter or margarine
About 2 tablespoons heavy cream or milk
1 teaspoon sugar
Sharp Cheddar cheese

Preheat oven to 425°F. Prepare pastry. Set out one 9-inch pie pan. Roll out the larger portion of dough and line pie pan; refrigerate remaining dough.

In a medium bowl, stir together sugar, flour, cinnamon, nutmeg, and salt. Turn into prepared apples and stir to blend. Turn apple mixture into pastry-lined pie pan; dot with butter. Take remaining dough out of refrigerator. Roll it to 1/4-inch thickness. Sprinkle a little flour over dough and cover top of pie with crust; seal and flute. Cut slits in the top crust to allow steam to escape. Brush top crust with cream or milk; sprinkle with sugar.

Bake until crust is brown and juice begins to bubble through the slits in the crust, about 40 to 45 minutes. When done, set out on a rack to cool for about an hour. Serve lukewarm or cold with generous slices of sharp Cheddar cheese.

81

The Pioneer Lady's Hearty Winter Cookbook

Pastry for Two-Crust Pie

2 cups all-purpose flour
1 teaspoon salt
³/₄ cup (1¹/₂ sticks) cold butter or
margarine

¹/₄ cup cold water

In a medium bowl, combine flour and salt. Cut in butter until the mixture resembles corn kernels. Sprinkle water over the mixture and mix thoroughly with a fork until all particles cling together to form a ball. Divide into two portions, one slightly larger than the other.

Jane Watson Hopping

Tit for Tat

I like the merry winter-time, with jolly ice and snow;
I like to pelt the little girls with snowballs as they go;
I like to see them dodge and run, and hear them squeal in dread;
I like to push them into drifts and scrub their faces red.

. . . .

But say, this isn't nice a bit! I've had about enough.
The winter is no fun at all when girls will play so rough!

—Annie Willis McCullough

In Jolly Wintertime with Jolly Ice and Snow

When our children were small, we bundled them up in fleece-lined coats, boots, and matching home-knitted scarves, mittens, and hats for rides out into nature's beauty. We scrambled into the old pickup truck and drove high into the mountains to marvel at the tall Douglas fir trees and the cedar, all draped in ermine blankets of snow. Then we drove down to see how the winter weather had changed the lakes we dove and splashed in during hot summer days. We got out of the truck and walked down close to the ice-covered water.

Because of the cold, we soon returned to the truck. The children wanted their father to build a fire so they could warm themselves and have something to eat. I set Mama's old cast-iron camping kettle on a rack over a circle of rocks and reheated a gallon of homemade chili.

Soon everyone settled down by the fire to warm their hands and feet. Randy told us that when he got bigger he would learn to ski and skate on ice.

Jane Watson Hopping

Colleen was more interested in the wintertime picnic. She impatiently waited for the cookies she knew I had tucked into the picnic box.

After we ate, the children built a snowman. Their father helped them a bit, but when Randy took off his new scarf and decided to leave it with the snowman, his father persuaded him to keep it for himself. "After all," he said, "there are many winter days yet to go."

By the time we arrived home, the children were complaining about the cold and their grumbling tummies that were empty again—ready for a cup of hot tomato soup and a cookie or two.

Mother's Homemade Tomato Soup

MAKES 4 TO 6
SERVINGS

When I was a little girl, about eight or ten years of age, I used to help Mother peel and can great boxes of tomatoes for winter use. Sometimes we put up as many as a hundred quarts. In winter, when fresh vegetables were not available or too expensive for a Depression-era family, we ate them right out of the Ball jars. We just put a little homemade mayonnaise on them and they became quick, delicious salads. Mother stewed them to eat plain and made sweet breaded tomatoes and this old-time tomato soup.

4 cups (1 quart) whole fresh or canned tomatoes
1/4 cup (1/2 stick) butter or margarine
1 large yellow winter onion, peeled and chopped

1/4 cup all-purpose flour
2 teaspoons salt
Freshly ground black pepper to taste
2 cups milk

Place the tomatoes in a medium saucepan. Break up the large pieces with a spoon. (Sometimes Mother worked them into a puree with her hand.) Set the pan over low heat and cook slowly for 10 minutes or more. In a large soup pot or Dutch oven, melt the butter. Add the onion and sauté until lightly colored but not brown, about 5 minutes. Blend in flour, salt, and pepper; slowly stir in the milk. Cook over low heat, stirring constantly, until sauce thickens and boils, about 1 minute. Stir heated tomatoes slowly into the sauce (not sauce into tomatoes, which may cause curdling). Cook about 3 minutes more over low heat to blend flavors. Do not boil. Homemade tomato soup tends to curdle.

Jane Watson Hopping

Old-Fashioned Butterscotch Refrigerator Cookies

MAKES 5 DOZEN
COOKIES

Colleen and I love to make these cookies on cloudy or rainy days. Soon, the day seems a little brighter. The kitchen smells good, and there's plenty of time for chatting. The menfolk drop in even more frequently than usual, and they leave in good humor after having consumed large handfuls of cookies and hot coffee or icy milk.

3¹/₂ cups all-purpose flour, sifted before measuring
1 teaspoon baking soda
1 teaspoon cream of tartar
1 teaspoon salt
1 cup (2 sticks) butter or margarine, softened at room temperature

2 cups firmly packed light brown sugar
3 eggs, unbeaten
1 teaspoon vanilla extract
1 cup finely chopped walnuts

Sift flour with soda, cream of tartar, and salt. In a large bowl, cream butter and brown sugar together. Add whole eggs, one at a time, beating well after each addition. Add vanilla and stir to incorporate. Then stir the flour mixture gradually into the sugar mixture. Fold in nutmeats. Shape dough into oblong rolls, wrap tightly in waxed paper, and place in refrigerator until firm, an hour or more.

About 20 minutes before baking, preheat oven to 400°F. When the dough is firm, remove from refrigerator and slice ¹/₈ inch to ¹/₄ inch thick. Bake until firm to the touch and lightly browned, 10 to 12 minutes. Remove baked cookies, one batch at a time, from oven, and transfer while hot to a wire rack or brown paper to cool. When thoroughly cool, store in airtight container.

NOTE: We put one or two dozen cookies in gallon plastic freezer bags and secure the top with a wire twist. When company comes, or when the men need a little sweet for their lunch, we whip a bag of cookies out of the freezer and in seconds have a ready-made dessert.

87

Ice-Yachting

Since ancient times, men have used wind and sail power to speed across the ice in boats on runners. The sport is popular in most northern countries of the world.

The first ice yacht in America was built by Oliver Booth in 1790. Ice-yachting contests were held that year on the Hudson River. The original iceboat was a simple square box fitted with ordinary skates on each side and one at the back, which served as a rudder.

Raymond's ancestors were English yeomen who during the Colonial period settled on the East Coast. Among family stories are a few about buying and selling land and boating on the Hudson River in summer and ice-yachting in the dead of winter.

On the Shrewsbury River in 1885, Commodore James B. Weaver, in his ice yacht, reached a speed of 107 miles per hour, which was the fastest speed that man had traveled up to that time.

Jane Watson Hopping

Great-Aunt Mae's New England Clam Chowder

MAKES 18 TO 24 SERVINGS

Among the recipes Ada's great-aunt Mae shared with the women of her family was this one for old-fashioned clam chowder. It was so well liked that family and friends gathered often in winter at Ada's house just for a bowl of Aunt Mae's clam chowder.

Ocean clams are grown in the cool waters of the North Atlantic.

3-pound, 3-ounce can of chopped ocean clams (Gorton's preferred)
2/3 cup butter or margarine
3 large winter cooking onions, peeled and chopped
8 large baking potatoes, peeled and diced

4 cups (1 quart) milk
2 cups light cream
Salt and freshly ground black pepper to taste
1/2 cup flour or cornstarch for thickening chowder (optional)

Drain the clams into a medium bowl, reserving the liquid. In a heavy skillet melt butter; add onions and sauté until translucent. Turn into a large saucepan or soup pot. Add potatoes and clam liquid. Cover and simmer until potatoes are tender, about 15 minutes. Add clams. Cook 3 minutes. Add 3 cups water and the milk; heat but do not boil. Stir in light cream; season with salt and pepper. Thicken, if you wish, with flour or cornstarch.

Adjust heat to serving temperature. Serve immediately with crisp oyster crackers.

Sunshine and Laughter

A laugh is just like sunshine.
It freshens all the day,
It tips the peak of life with light,
And drives the clouds away.
The soul grows glad that hears it
And feels its courage strong:
A laugh is just like sunshine
For cheering folks along.

A laugh is just like music.
It lingers in the heart,
And where its melody is heard
The ills of life depart;
And happy thoughts come crowding
Its joyful notes to greet:
A laugh is just like music
For making living sweet.

—Otto Arthur Morton, *Best Loved Unity Poems*

Jane Watson Hopping

Hooten Annie!

When I was a little girl, our family and their friends got together on wintry Saturday evenings for a Hooten Annie. Everyone we knew came, bringing the children and babies and carrying large bowls of food and canning kettles full of cookies and rolls. All who could play instruments, sing folk songs, or call for square dancing were especially welcome. Those who came with guitars, banjos, and other instruments were not asked to bring anything additional for the potluck.

My sister, Sheila, who now plays with the Grass Valley Symphonic Orchestra, still loves to play the fiddle with bluegrass bands and joyfully recalls those wonderful Saturday nights of our childhood when we stayed up so late dancing around the edges of the floor. As a matter of fact, it was midnight when we finally sat with adults at the groaning supper table.

A Winter Songfest

Music has always been a vital part of our family life. All through childhood, our old folk, parents, aunts, and uncles still played hill-country music on guitars, banjos, and fiddles. We grew up to the sweet sound of singing and joyful dancing to homemade music. Even today I can hear Uncle Ben picking and singing in a rich voice while we all sat by the fire, joining in now and again.

Sheila and I particularly liked to hear him sing "Woodman Spare That Tree":

> Woodman, spare that tree!
> Touch not a single bough.
> In youth it sheltered me,
> And I'll protect it now.
> 'Twas my forefather's hand
> That placed it near his cot;
> There, woodman, let it stand,
> Thy axe shall harm it not!

92

Jane Watson Hopping

That old familiar tree,
Whose glory and renown
Are spread o'er land and sea,
And would'st thou hew it down?
Woodman, forbear thy stroke!
Cut not its earth-bound ties;
O, spare that aged oak,
Now towering to the skies!

—George Perkins Morris

Of all the songfests, we children loved the Christmas gathering best. We all wore our good clothes, and our hair was combed into curls, to which our mothers fastened ribbons. Aunt Pauline played the piano while we all gathered around to listen to or sing "Silent Night," "O Little Town of Bethlehem," "Adeste Fideles" ("Oh, Come, All Ye Faithful")—which Aunt Mabel told us was our favorite—and other carols and old-time religious songs.

Afterward, we children would have cookies and milk in the kitchen while our families gathered in the living room to drink hot coffee, eat cookies, and share family business. By nine o'clock, we children were ready to go home. In the car, we'd settle down on our parent's lap, or in the back seat, and sleep until we sensed that home was nearby.

The Pioneer Lady's Hearty Winter Cookbook

Swedish Ham Balls with Honey-Mustard Glaze

MAKES ABOUT 75
SMALL MEATBALLS

When I was a child, my father had a reclusive old friend we called the Swede. I remember that he loved to play cribbage with my father and feed me smelly sardines and crackers.

Often he told us of his homeland. There are bits and pieces of his tales that I have never forgotten. "At home," he would say, "I lived in a red-painted log house. My father and older brothers were farmers in the eastern part of the country. On our forty-two acres they grew wheat, rye, barley, oats, potatoes, and sugar beets. In southern Sweden there is good grazing for cattle and hogs.

"Our mother often reminded us that our homeland has always been noted for its industrious, kindly people and for its good food. She and my sisters loved to set out our smorgasbord. The food was served buffet-style, each person helping himself to small portions of the many dishes provided." This was one of many delicious smorgasbord favorites he shared with us.

Honey-Mustard Glaze (recipe follows)
1 pound ground ham
1½ pounds ground fresh pork
2 cups dry white bread crumbs
2 eggs, well beaten
1 cup milk
Grated nutmeg for dusting

Preheat oven to 275°F. Prepare and set out a lightly greased 9-by-12-by-2-inch baking dish.

Prepare honey-mustard glaze.

In a large bowl, thoroughly mix ham, pork, bread crumbs, eggs, and milk together. Shape into small balls and place in prepared baking dish. Spoon prepared honey-mustard glaze over ham balls. Bake 1 hour, then turn ham balls over and bake at least 1 hour more.

Remove from oven, dust with nutmeg, and serve immediately.

94

Jane Watson Hopping

Honey-Mustard Glaze

½ cup honey
1 tablespoon butter

1 tablespoon prepared mustard,
natural stone-ground preferred

In a small saucepan, heat honey, ½ cup water, butter, and mustard together.
Cook only until a sauce is formed, about 5 minutes.

Ida Louise's Late-Harvest Jeweled Slaw

MAKES 6 TO 8
SERVINGS

By early December, all the garden vegetables, with the exception of kale and Swiss chard, have been harvested and laid by for cold-weather use. Frosts have killed the summer bounty. Aunt Mabel and Mother describe this salad as a midwinter pick-me-up salad that goes well with almost any meat dish.

6 cups shredded white cabbage
$^1/_2$ yellow bell pepper, cut into slivers
$^1/_2$ cup red bell pepper, cut into slivers
1 cup pineapple tidbits, drained
2 tablespoons chopped chives or sweet onion
$^1/_2$ teaspoon salt

Dash of freshly ground black pepper
$^1/_2$ cup mayonnaise
$^1/_2$ cup sour cream
$^1/_2$ teaspoon sugar
1 tablespoon vinegar
$^1/_2$ teaspoon dry mustard
$^1/_4$ teaspoon paprika

In a medium to large salad bowl, combine cabbage, slivered yellow and red bell pepper, pineapple, and chives. Sprinkle lightly with salt and pepper. In a smaller bowl, blend mayonnaise, sour cream, sugar, vinegar, mustard, and paprika.

Toss lightly with cabbage mixture and chill slaw at least 1 hour before serving.

Jane Watson Hopping

Easy-to-Make Dilly Rolls

MAKES 3 DOZEN OR MORE

I'm not sure who gave this recipe to Mother, but once she tried it, she loved it and shared the recipe with all the aunties and the young women in the family.

2 tablespoons granulated yeast
1 cup lukewarm water
2 cups (1 pint) warmed cottage cheese
¼ teaspoon baking soda
1 barely rounded tablespoon dill seed
2 tablespoons dried or chopped fresh sweet onion

2 eggs, beaten to a froth
2 teaspoons salt
¼ cup sugar
2 tablespoons butter, melted
6 cups all-purpose flour

In a small bowl, combine yeast with the 1 cup lukewarm water. Set aside until froth forms on surface.

In a large bowl, combine softened yeast with cottage cheese, baking soda, dill seed, onion, eggs, salt, sugar, and melted butter. Stir in the flour; beat with a wooden spoon to develop gluten. Turn dough out onto a floured surface and knead until smooth.

Wash the large bowl in hot water, dry thoroughly, and lightly grease. Return the ball of dough to the bowl, turn the dough to coat it, and let it rise until doubled in bulk, 45 minutes or more.

When dough is well risen, preheat oven to 350°F. Set out and thoroughly grease two baking sheets. Turn the dough gently onto a lightly floured surface. Shape into balls the size of a small lemon. Place close together on prepared baking sheets. Let rise once more until doubled in bulk, 30 to 45 minutes. When rolls are very light and give easily to a light touch, put them in the oven and bake until well risen and lightly browned on both tops and bottoms, about 15 minutes.

97

Little Benny's Red Flannel Long Underwear

Mother loved to tell stories about her favorite brother, Benny, who was about two years younger than she. Benny was full to overflowing with a zest for living and kept everyone laughing at his wild antics. One fun-filled story is about the time everyone in mother's family got new clothes for winter:

In 1911, farm folk didn't get something new every day. So when the boxes of winter clothes from Sears Roebuck arrived via parcel post, there was a great deal of excitement. Ben chattered and danced around the house until he made the old folks nervous. His mother told him to settle down, set by the window, and watch for his older brother Arch to come through the gate.

"Going to School" by Allen G. Miller, age 16. (Gold badge.)

Jane Watson Hopping

While waiting for Arch, the children took turns washing up so they'd be ready when the boxes arrived and were opened and the new things taken out and tried on for size. Even the old folks spruced up for the occasion. Grandma Meekins talked incessantly about the new piece of calico she had ordered, and Grandpa Peak told everyone how much he needed his new red handkerchiefs.

In time, the children let out squeals of delight as Arch drove the wagon, loaded with boxes, into the yard. To hasten the opening of the packages, Mother's father and the younger boys had done not only their own chores but Arch's chores too. In the house, women and girls fixed an easy supper. After everyone was fed, Mother's oldest sister, Mabel, and Grandma Meekins washed and put away the dishes, swept the floor, and made everything neat as a pin. Arch and Great-grandpa Peak pushed all the living room chairs back closer to the wall and then sat down to wait. When all was finally ready, the boxes were brought to the center of the room.

When the first box was opened, Benny, about age four, charged with great expectations, clutched the first garment he was handed to his chubby little chest and begged his mother to let him try it on. She reminded him that he had to handle the new merchandise carefully and that no one could return anything, even if it didn't fit, unless it was in perfectly new condition.

Then she sent him off into the kitchen to put on his new garment. Only a glimmer of light shone through the door and into the dark kitchen. The coal oil lamps had already been snuffed out to save on fuel. In minutes, Benny came flying back out of the kitchen and ran over to his grandpa to show off his new clothes. "Grandpa, Grandpa," he said, "you need some of these. They fit so good and they're so warm!" Turning 'round and 'round, he demonstrated the good fit, and bragging, he rubbed his hands over the soft fabric and neat trapdoor.

By then the whole family was laughing. In his excitement and hurry in the dark, Benny had put his new red flannel long underwear on crosswise. But undaunted, Benny didn't stop to pout or cry; he just went on with his high-

powered sales pitch to his grandfather.

Music

He plays the piano
beside the window
between firelight
and snow.
The old tunes.
Children
held by his children
in the warmth of winter glow
listen.

—Alvin Reiss

Cold-Weather Company

Uncle Bud and Aunt Sue loved to have their neighbors, church friends, and family drop by on chill, wintry days. Aunty's kitchen welcomed them with the fragrance of just-baked cookies, hot coffee, and tea. "Make yourself to home," they would say, and, "Sit down here!" and "That little punkin is no trouble at all." If the baby cried, Uncle Bud was the first to take it from its mother and rock it in the strong cradle of his arms.

Male conversations soon became loud and boisterous, and the men's laughter warmed the room. Women began to gossip, laugh, and tell humorous stories about one another. A few bustled about the kitchen, making batter for more cookies, filling the coffeepot, making some more tea. Others offered to help stitch on a large quilt Aunt Sue was making. Glad for the offer of help, she took them to the spare bedroom

A Bit of Sunshine

and called Uncle Bud to come build up the fire and help her let the quilting frames down to a comfortable height. She gathered chairs for the women and set out a small table for their coffee or tea and a plate of cookies. Then she went back to the kitchen to help the women there.

The children who could not wait to go outside and play in the snow began to nag and look for the coats, hats, scarves, and boots they had brought in with them. Older children played cards and guessing games. By lunchtime, the women had roasts in the oven, fresh bread made, and vegetables peeled, cut, and cooked. There was a steaming platter of fresh pork chops, and a pie or two as well. Tantalized by kitchen fragrances, the men wandered in and out, peeking into the oven or the large kettles that sat on the stove. "Stay for supper," Uncle Bud called out. "It's mighty cold out there!" Some folks who lived quite a distance away agreed to stay for supper, and some even took up the invitation to stay the night. Aunt Sue told them all, "Daylight will come soon enough, and that will make the trip home safer, particularly for old folk and children."

Ada's Pork Tenderloin Bathed in Sour Cream

~

When nighttime temperatures dropped almost to freezing, the men in Ada's family butchered full-grown, but not fat, hogs for winter meat. Men, women, and children pitched in to carry buckets of water, and tubs that would be filled with meat.

Sometimes neighbors came by to help with lifting and cutting up the meat for processing. Old uncles, fathers, and grandmothers all had good curing recipes. In no time, barrels would be filled with curing hams and bacons. The women would be busy making scrapple and panhaus, a molded mush made of broth and cornmeal. It is usually sliced, dipped in flour, and fried.

In those days, it was common practice to save out and cook up tender bits of meat, like the tenderloin, for children and old folks. This usually meant a great feast for all followed the work of the slaughter. Young and middle-aged folks helped the older family members and small children to settle around the table. With sharp knives, they cut the tender meat into larger portions for older folks and into bits for toddlers. Women scurried back and forth, bringing in more food, pouring milk for the young, and setting out pies or cakes that had been brought to the festivities. Old men and women bragged on the tenderness and sweetness of the soft, delicious pork made especially for them.

2 tablespoons leaf lard, rendered (see Note), or cooking oil
1 clove garlic
2 whole pork tenderloins (tenderloin is the little round muscle that lies opposite the loin in a pork chop)

Flour for dredging
1/2 teaspoon salt
3/4 cup sour cream

In a heavy frying pan, heat lard. Sauté garlic in fat until golden. Remove pan from heat. Cut tenderloins into 2-inch pieces. Dredge each piece in flour and brown on all sides. Add salt and 1/2 cup of the sour cream. Cover and simmer over medium-low heat until tender, about 40 minutes, being careful not to boil. Just before serving, stir remaining sour cream into the gravy. Serve with baked potatoes.

NOTE: Leaf lard hangs from the backbone near the kidneys. It is very mild in flavor and was used for making biscuits and crisp piecrusts.

Mother's Breaded Tomatoes

MAKES 4 SERVINGS

In the summer, Mother made breaded tomatoes with fresh vegetables. She cooked the tomatoes in a saucepan with nothing at all or a little bit of green onion. In winter, she used a quart of canned tomatoes for this dish. Grandpa, like other men of his day, spooned sugar over his until it was as sweet as a pudding.

We often ate tomatoes this way, for until we moved to California and had lived there for some time, we did not make Mediterranean dishes like spaghetti.

4 large tomatoes
Salt and freshly ground black pepper
   to taste

1 tablespoon sugar
1 tablespoon butter
$^1/_2$ to $^2/_3$ cup cubed bread

Wash, peel, and quarter the tomatoes. Put them in a pan with just enough water to keep them from sticking until they let out their own juice. When they are hot through and tender, add salt and pepper to taste. Add the sugar, butter, and cubed bread to take up the juice, and fold together.

Effie's Corn au Gratin

Everyone in our family and many of our friends grew corn, so it was a constant challenge to think of new, delicious ways to fix both fresh and home-canned corn. Effie found this recipe in a magazine, made the dish, and insisted we all try it.

Uncle Bud said, "Leave it to Effie to teach us a new way to fix corn." He ate several helpings to show her just how much he liked it!

2 cups tender yellow corn
2 cups dry bread crumbs
1 cup Cheddar cheese, cut into small
  pieces

Milk to cover

Preheat oven to 375°F. Grease a 2-quart casserole dish.

Put a layer of corn in the prepared baking dish, then a layer of bread crumbs, then cheese, and repeat until all ingredients are used. The top layer should be cheese. Cover with milk and bake until cheese is bubbling and top is light brown, about 30 minutes.

Jane Watson Hopping

Simple Hot Rolls

For years, Marge Mero, a longtime member of the local Grange, brought cloud-light rolls to potluck suppers. Needless to say, they disappeared in a flash.

2	tablespoons granulated yeast	1	tablespoon salt
$^1/_2$	cup warm water (105° to 115°F)	1	tablespoon butter or margarine, softened at room temperature
$1^3/_4$	cups warm water		
$^1/_4$	cup sugar	6–7	cups all-purpose flour

Dissolve yeast in the $^1/_2$ cup warm water.

In a large bowl, stir together the $1^3/_4$ cups warm water, sugar, salt, softened butter, dissolved yeast, and enough flour (about $3^1/_2$ cups) to make a sponge. Beat until smooth. Mix in enough additional flour to make a medium dough, one that is easy to handle. Turn out onto a lightly floured surface and knead until smooth and elastic, 5 to 10 minutes.

Place in a large, greased bowl and turn the dough to coat. Cover and let rise in a warm place until doubled in bulk, about 1 hour. (To test, touch the dough. If an impression remains when touched, the dough has doubled in bulk.)

Set out and thoroughly grease a large baking sheet.

Turn dough out onto lightly floured surface; knead 6 to 8 times. Pinch off pieces of dough the size of a large egg (if dough sticks to your hands, dust both dough and hands lightly with flour). Place rolls close together on greased baking sheet. Set rolls to rise again for 35 to 40 minutes.

About 20 minutes before baking, preheat oven to 425°F. Bake until well risen, golden brown, and firm to the touch. When rolls are done, bottoms and sides will be light to medium brown.

107

Wintertime

No matter that the pumps froze up
   and sleet slides in with the gale,
Folks gather 'round the kitchen hearth
   spinning many a memorable tale.

Popcorn dances in a wire basket
   giggled just above the coals
Next to the fresh churned butter
   sits hot chocolate and cinnamon rolls.

Mama, Papa, Rachel and Paul
   Virginia, Edwin, Billy and Gwen
All gathered together in love and laughter
   and joined by the bond of kin.

—Patricia Parish Kuhn

Jane Watson Hopping

Come a Hard Freeze

*Horses at the water trough
wait patiently for
grandpa's axe to quench their thirst.*

—30 Degrees Below Zero, Patricia Parish Kuhn

Midwinter on the farm brings an icy beauty to the landscape. Broken water pipes spray water over wire fencing to create a lovely, elaborate lacework, often thirty feet long. Trees dressed in ermine robes elegantly display their magnificence. Ancient pieces of farm machinery, like sculptures of old, remain in place, carrying messages of older days to all who admire them. They speak of the 1800s, of labor, of men and women who settled the West, of long-haired horses, and lean milk cows that trudged along behind the wagons, following the settlers west.

109

The Pioneer Lady's Hearty Winter Cookbook

Good Old Winter, When Kinfolk Stop by to Talk a Spell and Break Bread

Uncle Henry Beecher loved to stop by Ada's comfortable home to visit a while and sample her wonderful baked goods. He especially liked to stop in when Uncle Ned's buggy was parked out front and Uncle Bud and Aunt Sue's new Ford car was sitting in the driveway.

He'd knock on the door, and Uncle Bud would answer, "Hello, Uncle Henry. Come on in!" Uncle Bud would take Uncle Henry by the arm and, with a broad hug, would make him welcome.

Ada, knowing Henry as she did, told him, "Might just as well stay the day. Pretty soon there'll be pickin' and singin.'"

"A man could do worse!" Uncle Henry told Ada while he cut himself a thick piece of chocolate cake and asked one of the Lester girls to pour him a good-size mug of scaldin' coffee.

Families and single men began to drop by. In time, the parlor was filled with musicians playing "Red Wing," "Two Little Girls in Blue," "The Wabash Cannon Ball," "Red River Valley," and other favorite old songs. Sooner or later, the women would sing "Amazing Grace" and "Throw Out the Lifeline." Sometimes they'd choose to sing haunting songs about leaving the old homestead, or someone lost in the war between the blue and the gray.

Mama loved Uncle Henry and always made his favorite sweet—a Burnt-Sugar Chiffon Cake with Burnt-Sugar Frosting—for such get-togethers, just in case he turned up.

Uncle Henry's Favorite Burnt-Sugar Chiffon Cake with Burnt-Sugar Frosting

Uncle Henry thought this cake was perfect for eating in the winter, when he had his feet propped up near the fire. Mama thought it was a dessert cake but made it for him to snack on now and again. She felt this cake cried out for a generous garnishing of toasted crushed or broken pecans or of finely chopped walnuts, barely dry enough to put in the storehouse.

MAKES 8 TO 10 SERVINGS

2 cups sugar
1 cup boiling water
2 1/4 cups sifted cake flour (not self-rising)
1 tablespoon baking powder
1 teaspoon salt
1/2 cup olive oil or salad oil

5 eggs, separated
6 tablespoons cold water
1 teaspoon vanilla extract
1/2 teaspoon cream of tartar
Burnt-Sugar Frosting (recipe follows)
1/2 cup toasted pecans (instructions follow)

Preheat oven to 325°F. Set out a 10-inch tube pan.

In a heavy skillet over low heat, melt 3/4 cup of the sugar until clear and medium brown. Remove from heat and carefully add the 1 cup boiling water (it will splatter); stir until sugar is thoroughly dissolved. This will make enough syrup for cake and frosting.

Into a large bowl, put flour, the remaining 1 1/4 cups sugar, the baking powder, and the salt. Make a well in the dry ingredients and pour in oil, egg yolks, 6 tablespoons cold water, vanilla, and 6 tablespoons burnt sugar syrup. Beat until satin smooth.

Then, in a large bowl, combine egg whites and cream of tartar. Beat until very stiff peaks form. Then fold the egg-yolk batter into the stiff whites. Turn batter gently (so as not to lose volume) into the tube pan.

Bake for 55 minutes, then turn heat up to 350°F and continue baking 10 to 15 minutes longer.

Jane Watson Hopping

Remove cake from oven and invert pan over the neck of a bottle until cake is cool, about 1 hour. When cool, loosen cake from pan with a thin spatula or knife blade. Turn onto a serving plate. Frost with Burnt-Sugar Frosting. With a rolling pin, crush pecans into small pieces and garnish top of cake.

Burnt-Sugar Frosting

3 tablespoons butter or margarine, plus $^1/_2$ cup (1 stick)

3 tablespoons cake flour (not self-rising)

$^1/_2$ teaspoon salt

$^1/_2$ cup burnt-sugar syrup (from Burnt-Sugar Cake recipe, page 112)

4 cups sifted powdered sugar

4 tablespoons milk

1 teaspoon vanilla extract

In a medium saucepan, melt the 3 tablespoons butter. Remove from heat and blend in cake flour and salt. Stir in burnt-sugar syrup. Heat to a boil, stirring constantly. Boil 1 minute, then remove from heat.

Beat in alternately the powdered sugar and milk. Cream in the remaining $^1/_2$ cup butter and the vanilla. Cool and beat until of a spreading consistency. Spread on cake.

Toasted Pecans

Preheat oven to 350°F. On a baking sheet, spread pecans, halved and broken, in a single layer; bake 5 to 15 minutes, depending on size of pieces, stirring occasionally, until just lightly browned. (Nuts will continue to cook briefly and darken a little more after being removed fom oven.) Turn nuts out on brown paper to cool. One-half cup nuts is enough for garnishing the top of one cake.

Old-Fashioned Split Pea Soup with Deluxe Whole-Wheat Bread

~

MAKES 6 SERVINGS

When snow is on the ground, country folk sit by the fire, gossip, watch the kettles boil, and bring in a little wood to stoke the cookstove. Menfolk watch the women stir up this yeast dough and shape it into spongy loaves.

Sometimes neighbors drop in to praise the fragrance of baking bread that has filled the house and stay a while to share a chunk of hot bread topped with golden butter and a bit of summer jam or jelly.

2 cups dried green split peas
1 medium-size onion, peeled and thinly sliced
4 stalks celery, cubed
1 carrot, peeled and cubed
1 ham bone with meat still hanging on it
$1/4$ bay leaf

2 cups milk
1 cup thin cream (half-and-half is fine)
1 teaspoon salt
Dash of freshly ground black pepper (about $1/8$ teaspoon)
Minced fresh parsley, as desired

Rinse peas. Soak for several hours or overnight in cold water. Drain peas, then put peas, 2 quarts water, onion, celery, carrot, ham bone, and bay leaf in a large soup pot. Bring to a boil and simmer over medium heat until peas are tender, about $1^{1}/2$ to 2 hours. Turn off heat and let contents cool slightly. Remove ham bone and place on a small platter. Purée the remaining vegetable mixture until smooth. Return smooth mixture to the soup pot. Add milk, cream, salt, and pepper. Heat just to boiling point, but do not boil. Sprinkle with parsley before ladling into deep soup bowls. Serve with slices or bits of ham and Deluxe Whole-Wheat Bread (recipe follows).

Jane Watson Hopping

Deluxe Whole-Wheat Bread MAKES 1 LOAF

Mother has always loved this bread. It has acquired a flavor and texture that are the result of its having been passed down through an ancient family lineage. Great-Grandma Meekins called this bread the staff of life and dunked it in a deep bowl of soup.

3³/₄ cups stone-ground whole-wheat
    flour, unsifted
2 tablespoons granulated yeast
2 cups warm water (100° to 115°F)

2 tablespoons honey
1 tablespoon salt

Preheat oven to 200°F. Thoroughly grease a 9-by-5-by-3-inch loaf pan. Set aside.

Turn whole-wheat flour into a large mixing bowl; set in the oven to warm (both flour and bowl should be warm before stirring up the bread).

In a small bowl, dissolve yeast in ¹/₂ cup of the lukewarm water; stir in the honey and let proof. Add ¹/₂ cup more warm water and stir to blend. Remove warmed flour from oven. With a spoon make a well in the flour. Stir in the yeast mixture and enough warm water, about 1 cup more, to make a sticky dough.

Turn dough into prepared bread pan. Pat down with floured hands. Let rise in a warm place until increased in size by one third, about 1 hour. Preheat oven to 450°F. Bake until well risen, the crust is nicely browned, and loaf sounds hollow when tapped on the bottom, 45 to 50 minutes. For a crustier finish, turn off the oven, remove the pan of bread from it, turn out the fresh loaf, and set it on the oven rack for 15 to 20 minutes.

Effie's Sweet Winter Beets with Pineapple Tidbits

↶

Effie thought this side dish was more like a sweet relish than a vegetable dish. Whenever she was serving pork, cured hams, or sausages, she set this dish out in her mother's green bowl to show it off. Sometimes she garnished the dish with pounded blanched almond meats.

2 cups sliced beets, drained	$^1/_4$ teaspoon salt
2 tablespoons firmly packed light brown sugar	1 cup pineapple tidbits, with syrup
1 tablespoon cornstarch	1 tablespoon butter or margarine
	1 tablespoon lemon juice

Place beets in a saucepan. In another saucepan, over medium heat, combine brown sugar, cornstarch, salt, and pineapple with syrup. Stir constantly until sauce thickens and bubbles. Add butter and lemon juice; blend well. Pour hot sauce over beets and fold together. Serve hot or lukewarm.

Jane Watson Hopping

Warm Clothes in Vermont

Them flannel shirts we boys was wont
To don when days got freezy,
With bright, red braid all up the front
Where girls could see it easy;
Oh! they was warm enough to wear
Around the English Channel—
I wished today I owned a shirt
Of good, old, checkered flannel.

The seams and gussets, braid and bands
Was all to special measure,
And made to home by loving hands
That worked for others' pleasure;
Oh! if the tips of one was left
I'd make a splendid panel
And hang it 'bove my Claude Lorrain
To show that checkered flannel.

With sheep's gray breeches, copper toes,
And tippet warm and wooly,
Our clothes non-plussed the winds and snows
And did their duty fully;
'Twas human beings then that dressed,
Whilst pug and parlor spaniel
Got on, By Gum! with natural duds,
Unwarmed by checkered flannel.

—Daniel L. Cady, *Rhymes of Vermont Rural Life*

Winter in Vermont

During midwinter storms, our friend Henry Perry White worked his farm in Vermont. He kept the fires going, watered and fed the stock, mended harness, and carved wondrous ducks of every sort, wild Canadian geese, and other wild critters with his pocketknife. In summer, when tourists came around, he sold his winter-carved flock and many other of his pieces.

In winter, his wife, Gretchen, made fragrant pots of stew and delicious homemade breads. She knit all winter, making new sweaters, socks, hats,

Jane Watson Hopping

and scarves for Henry and the boys. She then made new shirts for them to wear when the weather broke.

Effie, knowing that Gretchen was housebound in winter, regularly wrote letters to her. The women exchanged memories, poetry, and recipes. In time, they became lifelong friends.

Broiled Cod Piquant

MAKES 4 SERVINGS

This taste-tempting dish is great for dinner at home or for taking to a potluck supper. It never has let Ramona Elrod down. Try it!

4 cod fillets
$^1/_3$ cup store-bought Italian dressing
Paprika

4 lemon slices
1 tablespoon capers
Sprig of parsley, minced

In a shallow baking dish, marinate cod fillets in dressing for 1 hour, turning only once. Sprinkle both sides with paprika. Broil 3 minutes on each side. Garnish top with lemon slices, capers, and parsley. Serve piping hot with baked potatoes and a green salad.

Change

Never an echo returns again
The perfect music of the refrain,
And never the silver of the rain
Glistens in selfsame showers.

The song, the singer, the echoes die,
The fresh clouds gather against the sky,
And man is privileged each morn to try
His will and reborn powers.

And never are days so dark, so sad,
But there are moments that change to glad,
And smiles are rainbows of storms we've had—
Tinted by varied hours.

—Grace E. Hall

Jane Watson Hopping

In spite of rain and reason
And winter on the wing,
My heart has its own season,
And my heart says it is spring!

- -From MY HEART MAKES ITS OWN WEATHER,
   James Dillet Freeman

Harbinger of Spring

In the northern half of the world, February hosts both cold, stormy weather and sunny days that seem to be harbingers of spring. The heaviest snowstorms of the year come in this sweet month, leaving the air crisp and clear and the earth covered with ice and snow.

Later in the month, there are breaks in the weather, and violets, primroses, crocuses, and daffodils color the landscape with pinks, butter yellows, and purples that speak of the fast-approaching spring and summer months.

Jane Watson Hopping

Sudden Showers

I know you are thinking of me.
The sun is longer.
Birds circle the almond tree
flying north.

—MESSAGES, Alvin Reiss

One of the things I love most about the fingerling valleys and mountain ridges of southern Oregon that surround us is the bright February skies that break into smoke-gray clouds. A light mist wafts over our mountains. It breaks now and again, revealing lingering snowbanks. The soft, misting showers that break into a minor rainstorm send everyone on the run to find shelter or an umbrella.

Shortly, a glorious burst of sunshine covers the sodden earth while fickle February revels in the light.

Quick-and-Easy Baked Sliced Ham

MAKES 4 SERVINGS

Uncle Bud raised lean pork and dearly loved the hams that he cured for winter use. Aunt Sue had her favorite recipes for turning the juicy, tender cured ham into special, delicious fruit-flavored treats for the family.

1 slice of smoked ham, 1 to 1½ pounds, cut about ½ inch thick
Whole cloves
2 tablespoons firmly packed brown sugar
2 tablespoons fine, dry bread crumbs (about ⅓ cup)

1½ teaspoons grated orange zest
½ teaspoon dry mustard
1 orange, cut into ¼-inch slices
Maraschino cherries, cut into rings
¾ cup orange juice, strained

Preheat oven to 300°F. Place ham in an 11¾-by-7½-by-1¾-inch baking dish. Insert cloves into ham; score at 1-inch intervals. Mix together the brown sugar, bread crumbs, grated orange zest, and mustard and sprinkle it over the ham. Arrange the orange slices on the ham over sugar mixture. Garnish with maraschino cherries and carefully pour orange juice over top of ham slice. Bake until lightly browned and heated clear through, about 35 to 40 minutes.

Jane Watson Hopping

Fruited Cabbage Salad

MAKES 6 SERVINGS

Effie thought this easy-to-make salad brought fruit and fresh vegetables to midwinter suppers. She often took a large glass bowl of this salad to cold-weather potlucks. Mama and Aunt Irene also began to make salads with sweet apples and various kinds of crushed nutmeats.

3 cups shredded cabbage
2 cups grated carrots
2 sweet apples, peeled and diced
2 cups chopped celery
2 cups pineapple tidbits, drained, juice reserved

1 11-ounce can mandarin oranges, drained
$1/2$ cup finely chopped nutmeats
$1/4$ cup mayonnaise

In a large glass fruit bowl, combine cabbage, carrots, apples, celery, pineapple tidbits, mandarin oranges, and nutmeats. Dress with mayonnaise thinned with the reserved pineapple juice. Generously serve in salad bowls or on salad plates covered with a leaf of lettuce.

Martha Washington Cake

MAKES ONE
8-INCH-ROUND
TWO-LAYER CAKE

Effie was the first in the family to celebrate George Washington's birthday with this special dessert.

Grated zest of $^1/_2$ lemon
$1^1/_2$ teaspoons lemon juice
1 cup sugar
5 eggs, separated
1 cup cake flour (not self-rising), sifted

$^1/_4$ teaspoon salt
Easy-to-Make Cherry Filling (recipe follows)
Whipped Cream Topping (recipe follows)

Preheat oven to 350°F. Set out 2 ungreased 8-inch-round layer pans.

In a large bowl, combine lemon zest, lemon juice, $^1/_2$ cup of the sugar, and the egg yolks. Beat until thick and lemon-colored. Sift the flour with the salt, $^1/_4$ cup at a time, over the sugar-yolk mixture and fold in. In a second large straight-sided bowl, beat whites until they are foamy; gradually beat in the $^1/_2$ cup remaining sugar. Continue beating until tips of peaks fold over slightly. Spread yolk mixture over whites; gently fold together. Pour batter equally into prepared baking pans.

Bake until well risen, light golden brown, and springy to the touch. When done, remove from oven; let layers cool for 10 minutes or more.

When cool, carefully loosen edges and turn each layer out onto waxed paper.

When ready to serve, remove waxed paper and transfer one layer to a cake plate, top side down. Spread half the cherry filling over the cake layer. Top with the second layer, bottom side down, and spread the remaining filling over the top. Top the cake with whipped cream or spoon whipped cream around edges of cake, leaving the cherry filling on top of the cake exposed. Cut 6 serving-size portions, and place them on dessert plates.

Jane Watson Hopping

Easy-to-Make Cherry Filling

1 21-ounce can cherry pie filling   1 teaspoon brandy extract

Turn canned filling into a small bowl; blend in brandy extract.

Whipped Cream Topping

1 cup heavy cream

Whip cream until stiff peaks form.

127

Sunlight and Shadow

The second day of February is called Ground-hog Day because on this day the groundhog or woodchuck is supposed to come out of its bur-row and look for its shadow. If the sun is shin-ing and it can see its shadow, the groundhog is said to go back into its hole to sleep for a while longer, indicating that winter is not yet over. If it cannot see its shadow, it begins its spring-time activities.

No matter what the groundhog did, at our house Grandpa started his spring planting of peas, potatoes, cab-bages, and other early crops on this aus-picious day!

Jane Watson Hopping

Old-Fashioned
Chicken Casserole

By February, women in farm country are butchering some of their larger birds for late-winter meat. Effie particularly liked to make this delicious old-time dish from her mother's recipe.

$^{1}/_{4}$ cup cooking oil (less, if desired)
4-pound chicken, fat removed, cut into serving-size pieces
Flour for dredging chicken pieces and for thickening
Salt and freshly ground black pepper

$^{1}/_{4}$ teaspoon curry powder (optional)
1 cup hot water
1 green bell pepper, chopped
2 cups peeled and diced carrots
$^{1}/_{4}$ cup hot water
1 cup milk

Preheat oven to 375°F.

Heat the oil in a large skillet. Dredge chicken pieces in flour and brown them in the hot oil. Season with salt, pepper, and curry. Place chicken in large casserole dish, keeping oil in skillet. Add the 1 cup hot water to the casserole, cover, and place in oven. Cook for about 40 minutes or until tender.

Meanwhile, sauté the chopped pepper and diced carrots in oil remaining in skillet. Add the vegetables to the casserole when the chicken is tender, cover, and continue cooking in oven for 10 minutes more. Add $^{1}/_{4}$ cup of hot water, as needed.

Remove chicken pieces from casserole, combine liquor from casserole with remaining oil in skillet. Stir in 2 tablespoons flour, and then gradually add milk. Continue cooking over low heat, stirring constantly, until smooth.

Serve with chicken pieces.

129

The Delicate Crocus Corners of February

*They slept, frozen
through midwinter
and now
awaken February
with the music of their dreaming.*

—CROCUSES, Alvin Reiss

Throughout our rural areas, there are old abandoned farmsteads that cling to the earth. Near barns and outbuildings, delicate crocuses thrust their heads through ice and snow to charm those who pass by. Great beds of them show off their multiplied beauty. Sometimes they share a spot with richly colored grape hyacinths. Violets throw their white, pink, lavender, and magenta blankets at the feet of ancient maple trees.

Pastel yellow-green buds, high in the trees, begin to unfurl. The sun sends pale-yellow rays toward the earth, promising warmth, color, and breezes that waft the scent of spring throughout the countryside.

Jane Watson Hopping

For Love Untold

We have a few treasured pieces of Grandma Hopping's Willow pattern, which was originally designed by an English potter to illustrate a Chinese love story. We read the lovers' tale from our cherished blue ware items—a small pitcher, a covered vegetable dish, and a plate or two. The story evokes visions of high romance.

Raymond, my husband, recalls sitting at the end of his grandmother's great oak table with its twelve high-backed chairs, waiting for her to serve his dinner on the deep-blue-and-white plates. While the two of them ate hot beef stew and biscuits, she would tell him again the legend of the old blue.

So she tells me a legend centuries old
Of the Mandarin rich in lands and gold,
Of Li-Chi fair and Chang the good
Who loved each other as lovers should,
How they hid in the gardener's hut awhile,
Then fled away to the beautiful isle.
Though the cruel father pursued them there,
And would have killed the hopeless pair,
But a kindly power, by pity stirred,
Changed each into a beautiful bird.
Here is the orange tree where they talked
Here they are running away,
And over all at the top you see
The birds making love always.

—OLD BLUE POTTERY, Ada Walker Camehl

Grandma Hopping's Old-Fashioned Beef Stew with Cloud-Light Dumplings

MAKES 6 SERVINGS

Uncle Vernon, as a young man, promised his father that he would watch over his aging mother. Almost daily, he would bring enough milk, eggs, fruit, and meat in from the farm to keep her freezer full. Regularly, she made this plain beef stew. If you dropped in to see her, she would ask you to stay and eat a bite with her. Always, she pulled out a bowl of ready-to-eat stew, warmed it, and served it with a bit of bread and butter. Sometimes she would insist on making dumplings, and often she had fruit on hand for dessert.

Everyone in the Hopping family knew that Grandma had a mind of her own. Raymond, who thought his dear grandma was getting old and a bit crotchety, asked her if she would like to go to the doctor for a checkup. Small and thin, stiff of back, her hair wrapped in a bun and her calico dress handstitched in her spare time, she told him: "No, Raymond! I don't want to see a doctor. All of my friends have gone to the doctor, and they died."

1½ pounds rump roast, cut into 1½-inch cubes
¼ cup all-purpose flour
1½ teaspoons salt
1 teaspoon marjoram
¼ teaspoon freshly ground black pepper

1 small onion, peeled and diced
1 cup chopped celery
3 medium carrots, peeled and cubed
2 large potatoes, peeled and cubed
Cloud-Light Dumplings (recipe follows)

Cut some of the fat from the meat and heat it in a large Dutch oven. In a medium bowl, combine flour, salt, marjoram, and pepper. Dredge meat in flour mixture. When part of the fat has fried out, brown the meat in it, stirring constantly. Add enough boiling water to cover meat and simmer until meat is tender, 2½ to 3 hours.

About 20 minutes before serving, add onion, celery, carrots, and potatoes. Add dumplings to the stew 15 minutes before serving. Cover the kettle closely and do not remove cover for at least 12 minutes.

Cloud-Light Dumplings   MAKES 6 TO 8 SERVINGS

2 cups all-purpose flour
1 tablespoon baking powder
1 teaspoon salt
$^{1}/_{2}$ teaspoon baking soda

1 egg, beaten
3 tablespoons butter, melted
$^{2}/_{3}$ cup buttermilk

Into a large bowl, sift flour with baking powder, salt, and baking soda. Make a well in the center of the dry mixture. In a small bowl, combine egg, butter, and buttermilk. Pour into the well. Stir just enough to form a heavy batter. Drop by $^{1}/_{4}$ cupfuls into hot stew or soup 15 minutes before serving. Keep covered for at least 12 minutes.

Speak not in anger. Little children feel
A million times more keenly than you guess;
You gain more quickly through a kind appeal,
And win to greater goals with a caress;
Ask not that babes shall understand each word—
The land from which they come is very still;
You, too, were years in learning what you heard,
And even now you err in good and ill.

—Grace E. Hall, MOTHERS OF BABES

Jane Watson Hopping

A Family Treasure

When young womenfolk brought their sturdy sons, lovely daughters, and small children to visit Great-Aunt Mae, Ada knew that eventually one or another of the little ones would tell Aunt Mae that she was four years old and that her sister Becky or Nan was three. Then she would ask Aunt Mae, "How old are you?"

Great-Aunt Mae would laugh and say, "I'm as old as the gray-green sea and the many-colored shells on the shore!" Ada would then gather the little ones about old Aunty's knees and settle them down while they begged for stories of sailing ships.

Later, the young folk put on sweaters and coats, perhaps scarves and mittens, and wandered off together to a sheltered spot along the beach where they spoke softly to each other. Boys touched the girls' long locks, dark brown with red glints, and talked about the work of the sea. They made a covenant with the girls they were growing fond of, written in the palm of their firm, raspy hands.

Late in the afternoon, with the help of the young women and Cousin

George, Aunty fixed a mighty-fine hot dinner, just what was needed as the

day was darkening to the sound of wind and rain.

Great-Aunt Mae's New England Boiled Dinner

MAKES 10 SERVINGS

Aunt Mae and her cousin George corned enough beef each year for midwinter meals. Their root cellar was piled high with potatoes, carrots, and beets. Before the weather got too cold, they pulled their cabbages up and shook the dirt off the roots. Then, with stout cord, they hung the heads upside down from the low rafters. In the off corner of the cellar, boxes and baskets of apples ripened and mellowed until they were all used up.

6 pounds corned beef brisket
6 small white turnips, peeled, roots and tops trimmed
6 to 8 medium-large potatoes, peeled
6 to 8 medium carrots, peeled and trimmed

1 medium to large cabbage, trimmed and rinsed
6 small onions, peeled and trimmed
6 beets, unpeeled, root and top left on

Place the meat in a large soup kettle; cover with cold water. Heat rapidly to boiling. Remove scum, reduce heat, and simmer until meat is fork-tender, 3 to 4 hours.

About 45 minutes before serving, skim fat from liquid. Cut turnips into quarters, potatoes and carrots into halves, and cabbage into 8 to 10 wedges. Add them, with the onions, to the kettle. Cook until vegetables are tender.

Meanwhile, place trimmed beets in a large saucepan and cover with water. Boil until they are fork-tender and the skin, root, and tops slip off the beets. Heat vegetables as needed to serving temperature. On a cutting board, slice the corned beef thin. Arrange vegetables, including beets, on serving platter around the meat.

Great-Aunt Mae's Indian Pudding

MAKES 8 SERVINGS

Great-Aunt Mae shared this recipe with Ada. When she came home from her visit East, she shared it with all the women in the family. Some thought it should be served in midwinter along with a New England Boiled Dinner. Some, like Effie, thought it a perfect harvest pudding.

4 cups milk
$^2/_3$ cup dark molasses
$^2/_3$ cup yellow cornmeal
$^1/_3$ cup sugar
1 teaspoon salt
$^3/_4$ teaspoon ground cinnamon

$^3/_4$ teaspoon grated nutmeg
$^1/_4$ cup ($^1/_2$ stick) butter or margarine
1 cup heavy cream, whipped or unwhipped, or 1 quart vanilla ice cream

Preheat oven to 300°F. Set out and thoroughly grease a 2-quart casserole.

In a medium saucepan, heat 3 cups of the milk and the molasses. In a medium bowl, combine thoroughly cornmeal, sugar, salt, cinnamon, and nutmeg. Stir cornmeal mixture, a small amount at a time, into hot milk mixture. Stir constantly while cooking over low heat until pudding has thickened, about 10 minutes.

Pour thickened pudding mixture into prepared casserole. Over the top of the pudding, pour the remaining 1 cup milk. *Do not stir!*

Bake 3 hours. Cool to lukewarm at room temperature. Serve warm or cold, each serving topped with 2 tablespoons heavy cream, several dollops of whipped cream, or a scoop of vanilla ice cream.

Jane Watson Hopping

The Girl in White

We saw her standing on our lawn,
One zero winter-day;
She never stirred, nor said a word,
Nor asked if she might stay.

And though it may not seem polite,
Indeed, almost a sin,
We never said a word to her,
Nor asked her to come in.

Her gown and cape and hat were white,
And white her feet and toes;
Her mittened hands were just as white,
And white her very nose.

She stood out there upon the lawn
All day, and all the night,
And never once lay down to sleep,
That stranger girl in white.

A dainty little maid she was,
A playmate you all know,
For she was "Jack Frost's little girl,"
Carved from the soft white snow.

—Charles Stuart Pratt

A Visit to Ohio

When Mama was a slip of a girl, Aunt Heta and her husband, Mr. Olson, lived in Ohio. In February 1910, Grandpa, Mama, and all her sisters and brothers boarded a train for Columbus, Ohio. When they finally arrived, Mr. Olson was at the depot with his wagon to meet them and help them with their baggage.

Aunt Mabel, who was Mama's older sister, had a few reservations about visiting relatives whom she had infrequently seen. When Grandpa's sisters had come to the Missouri farm, they had urged him to put his children up with relatives, which he had no intention of ever doing. The air was cold, and patches of snow lay everywhere. Aunt Heta had sent blankets with her husband for all of them to wrap themselves in. The ride to the Olson farm was a long and cold one. When they arrived at the farmstead, Aunt Heta and her small children were waiting in the doorway of a tall two-story house with richly colored window casings and doors.

Jane Watson Hopping

The inside was just as beautiful as the outside. Crafts of all sorts decorated tables and chairs. Handwoven, homemade rugs graced the floors. Tablecloths were embroidered, as were pillowcases and doilies in the bedrooms. Some pillowcases had two to three inches of crocheted lace on them. The comforters were filled with down.

Aunt Heta had fresh bread made, and meat was roasting in the oven. On the kitchen table sat fresh apple, homemade mince, lemon meringue, and dried-peach pies, along with several simple cakes the cousins had made for guests.

Early the next morning, Mr. Olson called all the children, just as daylight lit the sky. "Come," he said. "See what is on the grass!"

The children, still in their bathrobes, poured out the front door. On the lawn was a snow sculpture of a little girl. "This," he told Mama and the rest of the youngsters, "this is for you. Welcome to Ohio!"

Chocolate Snow
Ice Cream

Aunt Heta thought we children should have the pleasure of chocolate snow ice cream. She brought out unsweetened chocolate for melting, something we had never seen in our lives. She asked Mr. Olson and Grandpa to wade out to look for a deep drift of snow. They found one, brushed off the top layer of snow, then dipped a cup of snow out of the clean center, without dipping the cup deep enough to pick up dirt from the ground. They brought it to Aunt Heta for inspection, so that she could check it for cleanliness and texture.

Aunt Heta, convinced that the snow was clean and fluffy enough for ice cream, then sent her older children out to the snowbank with a large bowl into which they were to scoop up about 4 cups of perfectly clean snow, and pack it, covered, in a snowbank while still frozen. Meanwhile, in the kitchen, her older daughter whipped 1 cup heavy cream. She then folded some sugar and a small amount of melted chocolate or chocolate syrup into the whipped cream. She then sent her brother Roy to retrieve the covered bowl of snow. When he brought it in, she wiped the top off and removed it, then folded the snow into the cream-chocolate mixture, and added sugar and vanilla to taste.

Jane Watson Hopping

Aunt Heta brought out dessert dishes and served the snow ice cream by itself or with pie or cake, as desired, while still hardened. NOTE: If the snow ice cream begins to melt, cover it again and bury it in a snowbank until it hardens up again.

And whether it be the love we've won
Or the love that we have lost,
We value nothing so much as love
Because of its certain cost!

—From THE PRICE OF LOVE, Grace E. Hall

Valentine's Day: The Kingdom of Hearts

February 14 is a day on which gifts and romantic notes are sent and received. It is named in honor of St. Valentine, a bishop or pope of Rome.

One early authority, Bailey's English Dictionary (1721), says of St. Valentine's Day: "About this time of year birds choose their mates, and probably thence came the custom of young men and maidens choosing Valentines or special loving friends on that day."

In the days of quill pens, amorous swains were obliged to content themselves with sending their fair and chosen ones thick sheets of gilt-edged paper with gilt cupids carefully gummed thereon, and with the message about the rose being red, the violet blue, sugar being sweet, and so forth. All of which was written with an abundance of pen flourishes.

Jane Watson Hopping

A Valentine Rare

On Valentine's Day in 1947, Rob's wife, Emily, gave him a handwritten message: "Rob, this is the valentine my mother gave my father many years ago. It's faded, but the love they've shared has never dimmed. I give it to you because I love you and the children so."

When Jack showed the old valentine to his mother, Ida Louise, she cried. Tears of gladness streamed down her face as she kissed her beloved daughter-in-law, the woman who had filled her son Rob's life with love and happiness.

Emily's Valentine Cake

Young women in our family often made this colorfully topped cake and gave it to an admirer along with a valentine that invited him to come to her house for dinner on a Sunday afternoon.

2 cups cake flour (not self-rising)	2 eggs, beaten to a froth
2 teaspoons baking powder	2/3 cup milk
1/4 teaspoon salt	1/2 teaspoon vanilla extract
1/3 cup butter or margarine, softened at room temperature	1/2 cup finely chopped walnuts
1 cup sugar	16 maraschino cherries, cut into eighths

Preheat oven to 375°F. Set out and lightly grease an 8-by-8-by-2-inch cake pan.

Into a medium bowl, sift flour with baking powder and salt.

In a larger bowl, cream butter with sugar until light. Add eggs and beat well.

In a small bowl, mix the milk and vanilla.

Add flour mixture to the butter mixture alternately with combined milk and vanilla, a small amount at a time, beating after each addition, until a smooth batter is formed. Pour batter into prepared pan. Sprinkle nuts and cherries over top.

Bake until well risen, lightly browned, and firm to the touch, about 1 hour.

NOTE: When nuts and cherries are finely chopped, they will readily cling to the top of the cake while it bakes.

Supper at Aunty's House

Aunt Irene had no children of her own, but we cousins all enjoyed her lively company. She was a beautiful, flashy woman who dressed well, was greatly admired by gentlemen, and taught us how to clean and trim our fingernails. When I stayed all night with her, she would make strawberry ice cream in her little ice cream bucket for us to snack on before we went to bed. On our birthdays or other occasions, she gave us cologne or toilet water.

I particularly loved the beautiful bookplates she gave to me to put in my books.

Aunt Irene's Stuffed Pork Chops

MAKES 6 SERVINGS

When I was about eight or ten years of age, I loved to have Sunday supper at Aunty's house. She was a fancy cook, and I especially liked her stuffed pork chops. She served green salads dressed with olive oil and vinegar, whipped sweet potatoes, and for dessert, a tall Red Velvet Cake.

On Valentine's Day, she placed lacy cards on each plate and insisted we read ours before we tasted the Coca-Cola in our glasses. She would then set out a clean glass for our milk, a simple gesture that amazed my little sister.

6 double pork chops	$3/4$ teaspoon dried thyme, crumbled
$1^1/_2$ cups whole-kernel corn	1 tablespoon grated onion
$1^1/_2$ cups dry whole-wheat bread crumbs	1 cup peeled, cored, and diced apple
$3/_4$ teaspoon salt	1 egg
$1/_4$ teaspoon freshly ground black pepper	3 tablespoons milk
$1^1/_2$ tablespoons minced parsley, plus sprigs for garnishing	About 3 tablespoons fat, for browning chops

Set out a large frying pan. Preheat oven to 350°F.

Prepare chops. Cut a pocket on the meat side of each chop. In a medium to large bowl, blend corn, bread crumbs, salt, pepper, parsley, thyme, onion, apple, egg, and milk. Stuff each chop with corn mixture. Brown chops on each side in 3 tablespoons of fat; add $1/_4$ cup water—more or less, as needed—and bake chops until tender, about 1 hour. When done, remove from oven and place on a platter garnished with sprigs of parsley. Serve with a green salad and vegetable of choice.

Jane Watson Hopping

California Green Salad with Olive Oil and Vinegar Dressing

MAKES 8 TO 10 SERVINGS

When I was a girl, the only vegetables available during the winter were cabbage and carrots, sometimes celery, turnips, rutabagas, and the like. Lettuce and other assorted greens were not available, so Mother and the aunties made this green salad. It is still a lovely dish and one I love to serve even though we do have the luxury of greens year-round.

1 pound cooked green peas (canned salad peas can be used)
1 pound cooked French-style green beans (canned French-cut green beans can be used)
4 green onions, sliced crosswise
3 stalks celery, chopped
4 cups shredded green cabbage
Homemade French Dressing (recipe follows)

Marinate vegetables overnight in Homemade French Dressing. Now and again, turn the vegetables in the dressing. Drain well before serving, leaving only a shine of oil on the vegetables.

Homemade French Dressing   MAKES 1 1/2 cups

1/2 cup olive oil
1/2 cup salad oil
1/4 cup cider vinegar
1/4 cup lemon juice
1 teaspoon salt
1/2 teaspoon dry mustard
1/2 teaspoon paprika

Measure all ingredients into a jar with a tight-fitting cover. Shake well to blend. Chill.

149

Aunt Irene's Shallot-Buttered Carrots

MAKES 4 TO 6
SERVINGS

Aunty always had pots of chives and herbs in her kitchen window. Being a city girl, she cooked a bit fancy—with herbs, garlic, and shallots. Grandpa and Uncle Ben teased her about her uppity little onions. Eventually, they bought some sets and planted a row of them in their early garden.

Much to our surprise, the menfolk enjoyed this different carrot dish. Mother and Effie thought it added a nice touch to a pork-based meal.

1½ **pounds fresh carrots, peeled (Try to find small carrots of uniform size; they'll cook faster.)**
¼ **cup (½ stick) butter or margarine**

¼ **teaspoon salt**
   Pinch of freshly ground black pepper
2 **tablespoons minced shallots**

In a medium to large saucepan, cook whole carrots in a little water, covered, until they are fork-tender.

In a medium skillet, melt butter. Add cooked carrots and sprinkle with salt, pepper, and shallots. Heat carrots through. Turn, now and then, to coat them with seasoned butter.

NOTE: Carrots may be cut crosswise into 2-inch pieces or lengthwise into halves, as desired.

Jane Watson Hopping

Red Velvet Cake with Pink Mountain Frosting

For years, women in our family have baked this old-fashioned cake on Valentine's Day. Aunt Irene was the first to frost it with Pink Mountain Frosting.

MAKES ONE MEDIUM
TUBE CAKE

$^1/_2$ cup (1 stick) butter or margarine, softened at room temperature

$1^1/_2$ cups sugar

2 teaspoons vanilla extract

3 eggs, well beaten

2 cups sifted cake flour (not self-rising)

$1^1/_2$ teaspoons baking powder

1 teaspoon baking soda

$^1/_2$ teaspoon salt

1 teaspoon vinegar

1 cup buttermilk

$^1/_2$ cup unsweetened cocoa

1 tablespoon red food coloring

About 2 tablespoons boiling water

Pink Mountain Frosting (recipe follows)

Preheat oven to 375°F. Set out and thoroughly grease and flour a medium tube pan.

NOTE: I have one tube pan for angel food cakes and another one for cakes that contain fat, because light cakes made with whipped egg white will often fall if made in a pan that has been used for cakes with fat in them.

In a large bowl, cream butter, gradually add sugar, and cream mixture until it is light and fluffy. Add vanilla, stirring to blend. Add eggs, stirring well.

Into a medium bowl, sift flour a second time with baking powder, baking soda, and salt. Stir vinegar into buttermilk. Alternately add buttermilk mixture and flour mixture to creamed butter mixture, stirring well after each addition.

In a small bowl, combine cocoa, food coloring, and enough boiling water to make a thick paste. Let cool slightly, then add to cake batter and beat well. Spoon the batter into prepared pan.

Bake until risen, lightly browned, and firm to the touch, about 40 to 45 minutes. Insert a toothpick into top center of cake—if it comes out clean, the cake is done. Remove from oven. Let cake set in pan for 10 minutes, then turn cake out onto wire rack to cool. When thoroughly cooled, brush off crumbs and frost.

Pink Mountain Frosting

FROSTS TOP AND SIDES OF MEDIUM TUBE CAKE

$^1\!/_2$ cup sugar
$^1\!/_4$ cup light corn syrup
2 tablespoons maraschino cherry juice

1 drop red food coloring
2 egg whites (about $^1\!/_4$ cup)
1 teaspoon brandy extract

In a small saucepan, combine sugar, corn syrup, cherry juice, food coloring, and 2 tablespoons water. Cover and heat to a rolling boil over medium heat. Remove cover; boil rapidly without stirring to 242°F on a candy thermometer, or until a small amount of mixture dropped into very cold water forms a firm ball.

While mixture is boiling, beat egg whites until stiff peaks form. Pour hot syrup in a thin stream, slowly, over beaten egg whites. Beat rapidly until stiff peaks form. Add brandy flavoring during the last minute of beating.

Jane Watson Hopping

My Old Sweetheart

Each year on Valentine's Day, Uncle Bud gathered early-blooming flowers and gave them to Aunt Sue. He sang romantic songs to her and brought her pink and red ribbons to tie in her hair. Throughout the many years of their marriage, he told her that she was still as beautiful as she had been when she was sweet sixteen.

153

Uncle Bud's Favorite Red Cherry Pie

~

MAKES ONE 9-INCH PIE

In early summer, when cherries and apricots hang heavily on the trees, Aunt Sue picks and cans twenty-five quarts of red cherries for wintertime pie making.

After Christmas, now and again, she makes deep-dish cherry pies for her sweetheart. On Valentine's Day she gets very sentimental and romantic about her baking. She puts secret ingredients in the pies—a drop of red food coloring, a teaspoon of brandy extract. She also makes steam vents in the top crust with a tiny heart-shaped cutter that Uncle Bud made for her out of a tin can.

2½ tablespoons instant tapioca
1 cup sugar
4 cups (1 quart) home-canned red cherries, pitted and drained
1 tablespoon butter, melted

¼ teaspoon salt
Old-Fashioned Baking Powder Piecrust (recipe follows)
Heavy cream, for brushing piecrust

Preheat oven to 450°F. Set out 9-inch pie pan.

In a medium bowl, combine tapioca, sugar, cherries, butter, and salt. Let stand while pastry is made, about 15 minutes.

Jane Watson Hopping

Make the Old-Fashioned Baking Powder Piecrust dough. Line pie pan with half of the pastry, rolled to $1/8$-inch thickness. Moisten edges of pastry with cold water. Fill the pie shell.

Roll the other half of the pastry to $1/8$-inch thickness. Fold half of the pastry back on the other half. Place upper crust on filled lower crust. Open out folded half after it is in place. Flute edges. Brush top crust with cream. With a sharp knife, make several slits in the top crust to permit escape of steam. Or cut out small heart shapes.

Bake for 10 to 15 minutes. Decrease heat to 350°F and bake until pastry is browned and filling is bubbling.

Old-Fashioned Baking Powder Piecrust

$2^1/_2$ cups all-purpose flour, sifted before measuring
$1/_4$ teaspoon baking powder

$1/_2$ teaspoon salt
$2/_3$ cup cold butter or margarine
About $1/_3$ cup cold water

Sift flour a second time with baking powder and salt. Cut in butter until pieces are about the size of small peas. Add water, a small amount at a time, mixing lightly with a fork. Handling as little as possible, form the dough into a ball, divide in half, and form each half into a thick disk. Wrap in plastic wrap and chill until ready to use.

Pussywillows

We used to go the meadow trail—
A narrow path for two—
When pussywillows in the swale
Were softly bulging through;
And sometimes in your crinkly hair
I'd twist a furry bough;
The spring is here, but I can't bear
The pussywillows—now.

—Grace E. Hall

156

Jane Watson Hopping

Young Martha's Winter Tale

Aunt Clary's daughter Martha is still a skilled storyteller, even now, during her senior years. She loves to read colorful and fanciful stories to the children in the family who gather by the fire with her during winter. Sometimes Martha reads ancient tales, and sometimes she tells fairy stories she has written herself.

Dove-Gray Clouds Gather Against the Sky

Soft winter storms ride the wind over the mountaintops and into our valleys, leaving dove-gray mists hanging low, clinging to the tops of evergreen trees, wandering amid the madrone, maple, and oak trees, and through the low-growing Oregon grape and manzanita.

Horses with heavy winter coats stand in the doors of their stalls and beg for apples, carrots, and sweet flakes of hay. Inside the house, the family gathers for a little socializing. Women serve fancy little cookies and tea. Men and boys argue for hefty oatmeal cookies and steaming hot coffee.

Russian Tea Cakes

These delightful little snowdrops are perfect for a ladies' afternoon tea party. Women in the Southwest states call a similar cookie Mexican Wedding Cakes.

1 cup butter or margarine, softened at room temperature

1/2 cup powdered sugar, plus enough for coating baked cookies

1 teaspoon vanilla extract

2 1/4 cups all-purpose flour

1/4 teaspoon salt

3/4 cup finely chopped walnuts
   Powdered sugar

Preheat oven to 400°F. Set out a large ungreased baking sheet.

In a large bowl, cream butter, sugar, and vanilla together. Sift flour with salt. Using your fingertips, work the flour mixture and the nuts into the butter-sugar mixture until dough holds together. Shape dough into 1-inch balls. Place on baking sheet.

Bake until set but not brown, 10 to 12 minutes. Remove from oven. While still warm, roll cookies in sifted powdered sugar. Cool. Roll a second time until well coated.

Jane Watson Hopping

Life is a constant journey.
Never we reach the goal;
But the higher we go
*   the greater is the reach of the living soul.*

—From ADVANCEMENT, Claude Weimer

The Pioneer Lady's Hearty Winter Cookbook

When Early March Seems Middle May

When country roads begin to thaw
In mottled spots of damp and dust,
And fences by the margin draw
Along the frosty crust
Their graphic silhouettes, I say,
The Spring is coming round this way.

When morning-time is bright with sun
And keen with wind, and both confuse
The dancing, glancing eyes of one
With tears that ooze and ooze—
And nose-tips weep as well as they,
The Spring is coming round this way.

When knotted horse-tails are untied,
And teamsters whistle here and there,
And clumsy mitts are laid aside
And choppers' hands are bare,
And chips are thick where children play,
The Spring is coming round this way.

When coughs are changed to laughs, and when
Our frowns melt into smiles of glee,
And all our blood thaws out again
In streams of ecstasy,
And poets wreak their roundelay,
The Spring is coming round this way.

—James Whitcomb Riley

Jane Watson Hopping

In Like a Lion, Out Like a Lamb

I remember spring when I was a child. Grandpa would bundle up and dig in the cold earth. He'd plant peas and ready the rest of the plot for a later seeding of turnips, Swiss chard, beets, and other cool-weather crops. Then, as the weather warmed up, all of us—Grandpa, Mother, sister Sheila, and I—would pick crisp young greens and endless bowls of garden peas for Mother's canning.

Even today, if I close my eyes, I can feel the newly warm spring sunshine on my face and remember with my hands the shelling of a big bowl of peas. In memory, I can clearly hear the laughter and endless chatter. Mother would tell us children that the mind had permission to wander as long as the hands kept working.

No one really complained; we were all thankful for having fresh vegetables again. We ate peas in salads, buttered, in cream sauce, or combined with other vegetables. We greedily welcomed and ate all the other tender, young greens that were again available daily.

Jane Watson Hopping

Spring's Comin' 'Round

O March that blusters and March that blows,
What color under your footsteps glows
Beauty you summon from winter snows
And you are the pathway that leads to the rose.

—MARCH, Celia Thaxter

When the weather breaks in March, young and old alike take their horses out for a little exercise. Alone or with friends and family members, they seek out mountain trails and ride for hours, stopping now and again to rest the horses and have a bite to eat. All such folk that I know have a passionate love for giant firs, oak trees, wild violets, mountain lakes, and trout streams.

They speak of the fresh moist air, the scent of pine and wild herbs. Our son-in-law and daughter come back from such ventures in the wilderness refreshed, steeped in nature's bounty, and ready once again to deal with life's responsibilities.

Effie's Fruited Meat Roll

MAKES 8 SERVINGS

In early March, all the women would start complaining about not having anything but cured meat on hand. They would even begin threatening to butcher half-grown fry-ers, despite the fact that it would cut back on needed fresh chicken for summer suppers. So in the late winter the men in Effie's family often butchered pork and beef to please the cooks.

MEAT MIXTURE

1¹/₂ pounds lean ground beef
³/₄ pound unseasoned fresh pork sausage
2 teaspoons salt
¹/₄ teaspoon freshly ground black pepper (more as desired)
1 egg, beaten to a froth

STUFFING MIXTURE

¹/₂ cup dark raisins
4 cups toasted bread cubes, whole wheat or egg bread
¹/₃ cup minced onion
2 tablespoons minced parsley
2 teaspoons salt
¹/₈ teaspoon freshly ground black pepper
¹/₄ teaspoon dried thyme, crumbled
²/₃ cup soup stock or lukewarm water
2 to 3 tablespoons butter or margarine, melted

Preheat oven to 350°F. Thoroughly grease and set aside a baking sheet.

In a large bowl, mix together thoroughly the beef, pork sausage, salt, pepper, and egg. On a large piece of waxed paper, pat out meat mixture into a square about ¹/₂ inch thick.

To make stuffing: Rinse raisins, dry, and combine with cubes of toasted bread, onion, parsley, salt, pepper, and thyme. Moisten with soup stock, adding a little at a time, until softened but not wet. Spread stuffing evenly over meat mixture. Roll up jelly-roll-style, place on prepared pan, and brush with melted butter.

Jane Watson Hopping

Bake until meat roll is done, 1 1/2 to 2 hours. About 25 to 30 minutes before the end of the cooking time, set Effie's Sweet Potato Puff in the oven with the meat roll. Bake until puffy and brown. When done, serve meat roll and sweet potato dish piping hot.

Effie's Sweet Potato Puff

MAKES 4 SMALL
SERVINGS

2 cups mashed sweet potato
2 tablespoons butter or margarine, softened at room temperature

Salt and pepper
1/4 cup light cream
1 egg, separated

Preheat oven to 375°F. Set out a small to medium baking dish.

Turn mashed sweet potatoes into a medium bowl; add softened butter, salt, pepper, and cream. In a small bowl, beat egg yolk until light. In a medium bowl, beat egg white until stiff peaks are formed.

Stir egg yolk into sweet potato mixture. Then fold in the egg white. Turn mixture into a small to medium baking dish. Set baking dish in a pan containing enough hot water to halfway come up the sides of the filled dish.

Bake until puffy and brown, 30 to 35 minutes. Remove from oven and serve piping hot.

Aunt Irene's Broccoli with Hollandaise Sauce

MAKES 4 SERVINGS

Broccoli was not a vegetable commonly used in Missouri in the thirties. We learned to appreciate it in California, but that is not to say we all liked it. Grandpa never got used to eating what he called "green and yellow flowers."

2 pounds fresh green broccoli
1/2 teaspoon salt, or more

Hollandaise Sauce (recipe follows)

To prepare broccoli for cooking, remove the outer leaves, the lower part of the stalk, and any florets that do not look fresh. Chill the broccoli in cold, lightly salted water for a few minutes to kill any small insects hidden in its tightly wrapped florets—such pests generally float out into the water. Rinse the heads, checking for remaining insects. With a sharp knife, cut the stalks into quarters as far up as the florets. The object of splitting the stalks is to even up the cooking time between the dense stems and the soft florets. Lay the stalks in a large flat pan. Add boiling water and salt, cover, and simmer until tender. Broccoli should be eaten crisp.

To keep the color bright, leave the cover ajar.

Jane Watson Hopping

Hollandaise Sauce

This sauce takes special care to prepare, so have all of your ingredients measured and at hand.

$^1/_2$ cup (1 stick) butter
2 beaten egg yolks
$1^1/_2$ tablespoons strained lemon juice (or cider vinegar)

Dash of salt
Dash of cayenne pepper
$^1/_3$ cup boiling water

In the bottom of a double boiler, heat water until it is hot but not boiling. Into the top of the double boiler, put $^1/_4$ cup of the butter and the egg yolks, lemon juice, salt, and cayenne. Place top pan over the bottom pan. Stir until the butter is just melted. Immediately remove the top pan from the water and add the second $^1/_4$ cup of butter, stirring until the sauce is smooth. Add the $^1/_3$ cup boiling water, stirring constantly, and replace the top part of the double boiler over the water. Heat, stirring constantly, until the sauce is thick enough to coat a silver spoon (don't overheat, as it will curdle). Add more lemon juice if a tarter flavor is desired. If the sauce must be held for a while, pour the water out of the bottom of the double boiler, turn off the heat, and set the top pan back in place. Serve over broccoli. (This is a thin sauce; for a thicker version, add 1 more egg yolk.)

Aunt Margaret's Tomato Aspic Salad

Everyone in the family agrees that this is a delicious wintertime salad. At Aunt Margaret's, the tomato juice is usually home-canned, and the parsley is snipped fresh from a windowsill parsley plant.

$2^{1}/_{4}$ cups tomato juice
1 3-ounce package lemon gelatin
1 tablespoon cider vinegar
Dash of Tabasco
1 teaspoon minced fresh parsley, plus half a dozen generous sprigs to garnish serving plates

$^{1}/_{4}$ cup diced celery (center stalks preferred)
1 tablespoon minced sweet onion
2 cups (1 pint) small-curd cottage cheese

Set out an 8-by-8-by-1-inch baking dish. Bring tomato juice to a boil and dissolve lemon gelatin in hot juice. Turn off heat and add vinegar, Tabasco, minced parsley, celery, and onion. Pour into pan and let cool at room temperature. When only slightly warm, refrigerate to set.

When the aspic is thoroughly chilled and firm, cut into squares. Serve on a salad plate garnished with sprigs of parsley. Add a serving of cottage cheese to the salad plate.

Jane Watson Hopping

Mabel Meekins

By the sweat of me brow.
Aye, the sweat of me brow,
me brow, that's how!
By the good salty sweat of me
brow . . . That's how!

—Jane Watson Hopping

169

St. Patrick's Day

My grandmother planted shamrocks in her yard to be worn on St. Patrick's Day. For her it was, as it was for St. Patrick, an emblem of the trinity—the plant bearing three leaves from one stem. Green, the St. Partick's Day color, signifies the Irish people's undying recognition of him and celebration of his memory.

The Irish celebrate Sheelah's Day on March 18. One historian says, "Who Sheelah was is uncertain. Some say Patrick's wife, others say she was his mother, but all agree that the day must be celebrated, so the shamrock of St. Patrick's Day is drowned in the toast of Sheelah's Day."

St. Patrick is said to have been the originator of the right of the fair sex to propose marriage during Leap Year.

Jane Watson Hopping

Boiled Corned Beef

〜

MAKES 6 SERVINGS

Aunt Clary loved corned beef. She served it with generous amounts of boiled cabbage and skillet creamed potatoes.

3 pounds corned beef	Vinegar, 1 teaspoon for each quart of
1 carrot, scraped	water used for boiling
1 onion, peeled and left whole	Butter, as needed

Place meat in a large saucepan. Cover with cold water; let stand for 1 hour. Drain. To the saucepan add carrot, onion, and enough cold water to cover. Stir in vinegar. Set over high heat. Bring to a boil; reduce heat until broth simmers. Continue simmering until meat is tender, 30 to 40 minutes for each pound.

Turn off heat and let corned beef stand in broth for 20 minutes. Drain. Remove vegetables from saucepan and discard. Transfer meat to a large platter. Just before serving, rub with butter and slice. Serve with Old-Fashioned Boiled Cabbage and Skillet Creamed Potatoes (recipes follow).

Old-Fashioned Boiled Cabbage

Women of the past boiled cabbage until it was overdone and mushy. Sometimes they boiled cabbage and potatoes in the same pot. Our mother and grandmother cooked cabbage only until it was fork-tender.

1 medium-size head cabbage
1 teaspoon salt, or to taste
3 tablespoons bacon, fried crisp and crumbled, or 3 tablespoons butter

Freshly ground black pepper

Set out a large soup kettle. Cut the cabbage into narrow wedges. Place in soup kettle with a generous amount of water. Cook, uncovered, until fork-tender. Add salt to cooking water just before removing cabbage from heat. Drain. Season with bacon or butter. Add salt and pepper to taste. Turn into a heavy bowl and serve piping hot.

Jane Watson Hopping

Skillet Creamed Potatoes

MAKES 6 SERVINGS

Of all the women in the family, Aunt Clary was the most frugal. When she found potatoes in the cellar that had begun to wrinkle and sprout, she would pull the trailing green sprouts off them. She'd take the potatoes to the house, and prepare them for supper. First she'd boil them, then peel them, and then she'd cream them in a heavy skillet over medium heat.

2 tablespoons butter
2 cups peeled and diced cold cooked potatoes

Salt and freshly ground black pepper
1 cup milk
$^1/_2$ cup light cream or half-and-half

In a large skillet, melt butter; when hot add diced potatoes. Season with salt and pepper and almost cover with milk and cream. Simmer, uncovered, until milk is absorbed. Tilt pan occasionally and baste potatoes with milk. Serve piping hot.

New Holidays

At the Valley Glen School
paper silhouettes of George Washington,
of Lincoln, share the wall with valentines.
Small chairs shuffle in the classroom
and Miss Grundy, at the enormous age
of one and twenty,
stands over a circle of faces
not half her age
and reads of truth and cherry trees,
of a hunger to learn
so strong that the boy read by firelight
at night, and in the light of day,
split rails as lean as himself.

Beyond the room, in the halls, small coats
and rain hats and galoshes line the wall.
Outside, yellow buses wait in waning snow
to transport small dreams
of paper hearts and cherry pie.

—Alvin Reiss

Jane Watson Hopping

When the Sandman Comes

When we were children, my sister, my cousins, and I loved to stay overnight at each other's houses, to giggle and to all sleep together in the same bed. We told each other stories about elves and wild beasts and playing in the empty school yard. Those were simple days!

We could hear our mothers visiting in the kitchen and our fathers, and sometimes uncles, boisterously playing card games. When the wind began to howl about the house, or when we heard the hoot of an owl, we cuddled up even closer. One by one, we closed our eyes and sailed off to never-never land.

The Bounty of Childhood

In the country, farm folk reveled in the coming of spring. Soon there would be peas to pick, and potato sets to plant on St. Patrick's Day. Womenfolk longed for June, when red-gold potatoes could be grabbed out of the heavy-producing hills.

Women cleaned the storerooms and the potato and apple houses to see what needed to be used before the growing season began again. In the years of our childhood, Mama sorted the hard Arkansas Black apples that had set in her closet from December until spring. Daddy and Grandpa carried the burlap bags of apples out into our kitchen, filling the entire house with their heady fruity fragrance. Grandpa, who often helped, wanted Mama to make apple pies, and Daddy, who loved turnovers drizzled with powdered-sugar glaze, agreed to help peel the apples.

When there was a bountiful store of nuts, Mama made several batches of cookies and cakes with nuts in them. Sometimes she made a special treat, chocolate nut fudge.

Jane Watson Hopping

Pecan
Nut Drops

When Mother was a girl, she and her family took the wagon down into the bottom lands along the Osage River in Missouri to pick up wild pecans. They would sell them and store them for winter use.

After we had moved to California in 1931, she still talked about the richness of having pecans to bake with. The walnuts and almonds on our place never quite measured up to the nut-filled bounty of her childhood. This was one of her favorite recipes from childhood.

1 cup (2 sticks) butter or margarine, softened at room temperature
1 cup sugar
2 large eggs, beaten to a froth
2 teaspoons vanilla extract
2$^{1}/_{2}$ cups all-purpose flour

$^{1}/_{2}$ teaspoon baking soda
$^{1}/_{4}$ teaspoon salt
2 cups pecan pieces (halves cut into 2 or 3 pieces each)
$^{1}/_{2}$ cup shredded moist coconut
Candied fruit, for garnish (optional)

Preheat oven to 350°F. Set out one or two large baking sheets.

In a large bowl, cream together butter and sugar. Blend in beaten eggs and vanilla. In a medium bowl, sift flour, baking soda, and salt together. Turn flour mixture into butter mixture and stir until well blended. Fold in nuts and coconut.

Drop by teaspoonfuls onto the baking sheet. Bake until risen and lightly browned, 12 to 15 minutes. Garnish top before baking with glazed red or green cherries or other candied fruits, if desired.

A Winter Wonderland

Minnesota is known as "the land of sky-tinted water," the North Star State, and the Bread and Butter State. It is a state of eleven thousand lakes and the birthplace of the mighty Mississippi. Longfellow, the author of "Hiawatha," called it "the land of Dacotahs, where the falls of Minnehaha flashed and gleamed" and rivers rushed through "palisades of pine trees."

The dreams of thousands of Scandinavian pioneers came true when they reached the rich acres of the southern central and western parts of the state. Aunt Clary's oldest son married a beautiful blond girl named Inger, who went west with him. Sturdy, thrifty, industrious Swedes, Norwegians, and Danes stood up to the dangers of frontier life in their region. They built homes, brought brides from the old country, and cultivated the rich land in the Red River Valley. It soon bore wheat, potatoes, rye, hay, barley, corn, and flax. They also raised animals like hogs and poultry. And they wrote home, encouraging friends to share in their successes.

Jane Watson Hopping

Wild game and fish were abundant in the pine forests that towered and filled the air with their fragrance. In those early days, two-wheeled oxcarts were the chief means of overland travel, especially in the Red River Valley.

To this frontier, trappers moved in search of pelts, lumberjacks came and logged its lordly white pines, rugged men settled and plowed under the tough prairie sod.

Northern-born Scandinavians thrived in the healthful, bracing climate, from the milder northeast of the state, influenced by Lake Superior, to the coolest section in the extreme northwest. Snowfall in Minnesota varies from about 20 inches annually in the extreme southeast to more than 70 inches in the northeastern corner.

Mother tells a tale about her great-aunt Martha, who married a Swede from Minnesota and worked among the missionaries teaching Indian children.

Scandinavian-Born

From childhood on, Swedes love the sun and prefer to be outside as much as possible. Athletic to the core, they participate in numerous sports, which are an important part of school training. In winter, they are avid skaters and skiers. During the summer months, they enjoy swimming, boating, field and track, hiking, and camping.

Deluxe Split Pea Soup with Precooked Smoked Link Sausage

MAKES 8 TO 10
SERVINGS

Inger loves this spicy soup and in winter serves it often with toasted bread and a mixed fruit salad.

1 pound dry green split peas
1 cup coarsely chopped yellow winter onion
1 large clove garlic, peeled and crushed (or $^1/_4$ to $^1/_2$ teaspoon granulated garlic)
$^1/_2$ teaspoon crushed red pepper
$^1/_2$ teaspoon dried marjoram, crumbled

2 medium bay leaves
$1^1/_2$ cups coarsely chopped celery
$^3/_4$ cup peeled and coarsely chopped potatoes
1 cup cubed precooked ham
1 pound precooked smoked link sausage (or Italian or Polish sausage), cut into chunks

In a large soup kettle, cover peas with 2 quarts water, bring water to a boil, and simmer for 3 minutes. Remove from heat and let soak for at least 1 hour. Add the onion, garlic, red pepper, and marjoram. Bring to a boil and add bay leaves, reduce heat and simmer, covered, for 2 hours, stirring occasionally. Remove the bay leaves. Add celery and potatoes and cook over low heat 30 minutes. Add the ham and sausage chunks to the soup and simmer until both are thoroughly heated, 30 minutes longer. Serve piping hot.

A Delicious Cardamom Braid

MAKES 1 BRAID

The recipe for this holiday bread was given to Effie in 1937 by a Scandinavian neighbor. Through the years, she has shared the original recipe with other women in the family. Some of them have varied the ingredients, making a delicious braid of their own. I have always found this original recipe the most tasty.

½ cup golden raisins
¼ cup dark raisins
¼ cup candied lemon peel, plus more for decorating braid, if desired
¼ cup candied orange peel, plus more for decorating braid, if desired
¼ cup brandy (optional) (combined apple cider and 1 tablespoon brandy extract can be substituted)
3 tablespoons grated lemon zest
1 tablespoon lemon juice, strained

2½ cups all-purpose flour
2 teaspoons ground cardamom
1 teaspoon salt
¾ cup lukewarm milk (105° to 115°F)
2 tablespoons granulated yeast
⅓ cup butter or margarine, softened at room temperature
¼ cup sugar
2 eggs
Simple Icing (recipe follows)

In a small bowl, combine golden and dark raisins, candied peels, brandy, grated lemon zest, and lemon juice. Set aside.

In a large mixing bowl, combine flour, cardamom, and salt. In a small bowl, combine lukewarm milk, yeast, butter, and sugar. Let stand for 10 minutes to give yeast time to bubble up. Add the milk mixture to the flour mixture and stir to blend.

Beat one of the eggs into a froth; add to the raisin-brandy mixture. Add the raisin-brandy mixture to the flour mixture and combine to form a soft dough, one that is almost too soft to handle.

Turn the dough out onto a floured surface and knead until smooth and elastic, about 8 to 10 minutes. Cover and let rest for at least 10 minutes.

182

Jane Watson Hopping

Form dough into three 18-inch ropes. Braid the ropes together, tucking the ends under. Place on greased baking sheet. Cover and let rise in a warm place until almost doubled in bulk, 45 minutes to 1 hour.

Meanwhile, preheat oven to 350°F. Beat the remaining egg well and brush the braid with the beaten egg. Bake until well risen, light golden brown, and a bit firm to the touch. Remove from oven and transfer to wire rack to cool. While still warm, drizzle with simple icing. Decorate with additional candied fruits as desired.

Simple Icing

1 cup sifted powdered sugar

2 tablespoons milk, half-and-half, or light cream

Whisk until smooth and of spreading consistency.

From the Land of Used-to-Be

On cold, wintry days, Mama liked to settle down by the fire with Sheila and me and tell us of her own childhood. We loved it when she told us about Dear Ol' Popy, who we knew was our own dear grandpa, Mama's father, who lived with us.

We would beg and she would tease us before telling us once again about his wonderfulness:

> When I was a little girl, all of us children in the home called our father "Popy." He loved our mother and was playful with us children. He made swings and playing fields for us, homemade baseball bats and a ball. He took us fishing and called us in the night when a new calf was born. He would carry our little brother Fred out in his nightgown and talk to him about the miracle of birth.

Mother's eyes would mist up when she recalled the love and care he gave his family, exhausted though he was by the hours he spent farming. One of her favorite memories was of him singing and playing the mandolin in the evening. She told how she loved the old country ballads with the flavor of fifteenth-century England, Ireland, and Scotland still lingering in them, echoing the distant past.

Jane Watson Hopping

Sometimes, she would recall his sorrow when his children grew older and were embarrassed to still call him Popy. One after another, they began to call him Dad. She would go outside and look for her father, who lived with us, and she would tell him in many ways how important to her he had been in her childhood. Before she left us to play by ourselves, she would make us laugh by reciting this little verse for us:

> *And where's the land of Used-to-be, does little baby wonder?*
> *Oh, we will clap a magic saddle over Popy's knee,*
> *And ride away around the world, and in and out and under. . . .*

—From THE LAND OF USED-TO-BE, James Whitcomb Riley

Jane Watson Hopping

A Simple Recipe

To be a wholly worthy man,
    As you, my boy, would like to be,
This is to show you how you can
    This simple recipe:
Be honest—both in word and act,
    Be strictly truthful through and through:
Fact can not fail.—You stick to fact,
    And fact will stick to you.
Be clean outside and in, and sweep
    Both hearth and heart and hold them bright;
Wear snowy linin aye, and keep
    Your conscience snowy-white.
Do right, your utmost good must come
    To you who do your level best
Your very hopes will help you some,
    And work will do the rest.

—James Whitcomb Riley

The Making of a Man

One day at a livestock auction, I watched a nearby Scandinavian woman with several small children clustered about her. They were about the business of buying a calf to raise. The oldest child, a boy of eleven or twelve years, and the mother were discussing the breed of calf they needed and how much they would be able to pay for it.

Eventually, a number of month-old calves came bouncing into the ring. Out of her purse, the mother handed her oldest son a notepad and a pencil. She told him to go down to the fence that surrounded the arena, to pick out the three or four calves he thought would meet their needs, and to write down the numbers of the tags fastened to them. When he had written down some four or five numbers on his notepad, he came back up and sat down beside his mother. Again, they discussed the calves he had chosen, and she listened carefully as he explained just why he had chosen each one and in which order his choices were listed for bidding.

As the auctioneer began to ask for bids, the mother pointed discreetly to men who were already bidding. Leaning close to him, she said, "See how the men signal when they want to buy." Not only the boy but all of the children watched carefully as bidders called out the numbers on the tags stuck to the calves' backs. Intensely, the boy watched and waited for a price to be low enough so that they could bid on a calf. Finally, he put up his hand. The auctioneer saw him but didn't acknowledge his signal. The boy gave a second signal, and that time the auctioneer recognized his bid. The boy loudly called out the number of his choice, but a woman quickly outbid him. He tried again, only to be outbid again by a man across the arena. Then, on his third try, he got the bid and the calf that seemed to be the third choice on his list. He turned to catch his mother's gaze. She nodded her approval to him, but made no sign of exaggerated praise.

I could not help but think how wise she was, teaching her son and all her other children that all of us must learn how to do the necessary things and to meet our responsibilities in life without a big hurrah. Through the years, I have often thought of the woman of modest means, her lovely children, and her uncommon mothering skills.

Norwegian Vegetable Soup with Boiled Meat in Sauce

~

MAKES ABOUT
10 SERVINGS

The basic recipe for this soup is very old. This variation, which includes tomatoes, dates back to the mid-1800s, when love apples (tomatoes) were first accepted as a wholesome food. Until then they had been grown as ornamentals and were believed to be poisonous because they belonged to the nightshade family.

2 pounds beef short ribs
1 pound soup bones, with meat clinging to them
1 tablespoon salt
1^1/$_2$ cups coarsely chopped onion
1^1/$_2$ cups peeled and coarsely chopped carrots
1 small (1 pound) cabbage, trimmed and cut into pieces

1 whole nutmeg
4 medium tomatoes, peeled and stem ends removed
2 beef bouillon cubes (optional)
Freshly ground black pepper
^{1}/$_4$ cup finely chopped parsley
Sauce for Boiled Meat (recipe follows)

Wipe short ribs with clean, damp cloth. Put ribs and soup bones into a large soup pot or Dutch oven with 3 quarts cold water and 1^1/$_2$ teaspoons salt. Bring to a boil over high heat, then reduce heat and simmer. During cooking, occasionally remove foam that forms on top.

When soup has simmered 1 hour, add onions. Continue simmering 1 hour longer, then add carrots and cabbage. Simmer an additional 30 minutes. Skim off most of the fat from the soup, leaving about 2 tablespoons. Add whole nutmeg and tomatoes. Simmer 15 minutes longer, then remove from heat. Remove and discard nutmeg. With a slotted spoon, lift short ribs and soup bones from soup. Put them in a bowl to cool. When they can be handled without burning the fingers, remove meat from bones. Cut off gristle and other coarse material and discard. Cut meat into serving-size pieces and set aside until needed.

Jane Watson Hopping

Add bouillon cubes as desired and stir until dissolved. Adjust seasonings by adding about 1^1/$_2$ teaspoons salt and ^{1}/$_4$ teaspoon black pepper. Remove 2 cups broth for use in sauce. Stir parsley into remaining soup. Keep soup hot while preparing sauce for meat. When sauce is made, add the meat to the sauce and warm over low heat until both are hot.

Serve soup first, then serve meat and sauce.

Sauce for Boiled Meat

^{1}/$_4$ cup (^{1}/$_2$ stick) butter or margarine
^{1}/$_4$ cup flour
^{1}/$_2$ teaspoon salt
^{1}/$_8$ teaspoon freshly ground black pepper

2 cups broth (reserved from soup)
4 teaspoons sugar
2 tablespoons vinegar
2 tablespoons prepared horseradish

In a medium saucepan, melt butter and blend in flour. Add salt and pepper. When mixture is bubbling, remove from heat and gradually stir in broth. Return to heat and cook rapidly, stirring constantly until sauce thickens. Cook 1 to 2 minutes longer. Remove sauce from heat and stir in sugar, vinegar, and horseradish.

Norwegian Rye Bread

MAKES 2 LOAVES

When rye bread is made, the rye flour is usually combined with hard-wheat flour, whole-wheat flour, all-purpose flour, or a combination of the three, because the gluten in rye flour is insufficient to support the elasticity that allows yeast breads to rise well. This bread is moist and compact and has a sturdy, old-fashioned flavor.

1 cup whole-wheat flour
3 cups rye flour
$^1/_4$ cup firmly packed dark brown sugar
1 tablespoon salt

Hot water, as needed
1 tablespoon granulated yeast
$^1/_4$ cup warm water (105° to 115°F) for dissolving yeast, plus $^3/_4$ cup
About 2 cups all-purpose flour

Into a large bowl, sift the flours, brown sugar, and salt. Beat in enough hot water to make a stiff batter. Cover and let stand until lukewarm. Add yeast to $^1/_4$ cup warm water. Let set until frothy, about 10 minutes. Then add yeast and remaining $^3/_4$ cup warm water to batter. Add enough all-purpose flour to mold dough into a ball. Turn out onto surface coated with all-purpose flour. Wash bread-making bowl, grease it lightly, and place dough back in the bowl, turning it to grease on all sides. Cover and let stand in a warm place until doubled in bulk. (To test, touch the dough. If an impression remains when touched, the dough has doubled in bulk.)

Thoroughly grease $8^1/_2$-by-$4^1/_2$-by-$2^1/_2$-inch loaf pans. Punch dough down and shape into two loaves; place in prepared pans. Cover and let rise in a warm place until doubled in bulk. Preheat oven to 375°F. Bake until well risen, browned, and firm to the touch, about 1 hour and 15 minutes. Remove from oven, let rest in pans 8 to 10 minutes, then turn onto a wire rack to cool.

Jane Watson Hopping

Bubbling Soup Pots

Great-Grandma Meekins daily kept a nourishing soup pot simmering on the back of a big black woodstove. She thought such soup with a slice of bread kept workingmen and children strong and healthy. Her soups tended to be made with bits of leftover meat and vegetables. Grandpa preferred corn chowder seasoned with ham. The boys in the family liked vegetable chowders heavily laced with bits of leftover roast pork butts. The girls—Mabel, Gladys, and Hattie—liked chicken soups with noodles or rice in them. In late winter, Great-Grandma fancied bean and green or yellow split pea soups with toasted breads.

Grandpa could always persuade his mother or our own mother to make oyster stew or clam chowder in season. For such a feast, he would make a trip to town to buy crisp saltine crackers.

Old-Country Beef Stew with Southern-Style Sweet Potato Biscuits

～

On cold, blustery days, Effie loved to make her grand-mother's rich, chunky beef stew enriched with onions, carrots, and potatoes, and she served it with small, hot sweet potato biscuits with fresh butter and honey.

MAKES 8 OR 9
SERVINGS

2 pounds round steak
1/2 cup all-purpose flour
1 teaspoon salt
1/2 teaspoon freshly ground black pepper
1 teaspoon dried thyme, crumbled
1/2 teaspoon grated nutmeg
1/4 cup (1/2 stick) margarine or shortening
4 cups (1 quart) boiling water
1 tablespoon cider vinegar or lemon juice

1 tablespoon honey (clover honey preferred)
1 large onion, peeled and diced
Sprig of parsley
1 bay leaf
1 clove garlic, peeled and crushed
A dozen small carrots, trimmed, peeled, and cut in half
12 to 16 small, thin-skinned potatoes, scrubbed and halved

Set out a large, heavy pot or Dutch oven.

Wipe meat down with a clean, damp cloth and cut into 2-inch cubes.

In a medium bowl, combine flour, salt, pepper, thyme, and nutmeg. Roll cubes in flour mixture until well coated and shake off excess flour mixture. Heat the margarine in the pot over high heat; melt until hot but not burn-ing or smoking. Carefully add cubes of beef, a little at a time. Brown on all sides, moving pieces gently until all the cubes are well browned. Pour on the boiling water, being careful not to get spattered with hot fat.

194

Add vinegar, honey, onion, parsley, bay leaf, and garlic. Lower heat, cover, and simmer until meat is tender, $1^1/_2$ to 2 hours. Add carrots and new potatoes and cook until vegetables are fork-tender, 20 to 25 minutes. Serve while piping hot with sweet potato biscuits, fresh butter, and honey.

Southern-Style Sweet Potato Biscuits
MAKES ABOUT 16 SMALL BISCUITS

1 cup all-purpose flour
1 tablespoon baking powder
$^3/_4$ teaspoon salt
2 generous tablespoons butter or margarine

1 cup mashed sweet potatoes
2 to 4 tablespoons cold milk, as needed

Preheat oven to 450°F. Lightly grease a large baking sheet.

In a large mixing bowl, combine flour, baking powder, and salt. Rub in the butter using fingertips. Add sweet potatoes, then enough milk to make a soft dough. Turn dough onto a lightly floured surface; knead about 30 seconds. *Don't overwork dough.* Pat dough lightly into a rectangle $^1/_2$-inch thick. Cut with floured biscuit cutter about $2^1/_2$ inches in diameter.

Place on prepared baking sheet. Set in a very hot oven and bake until well risen and lightly browned, 15 to 20 minutes.

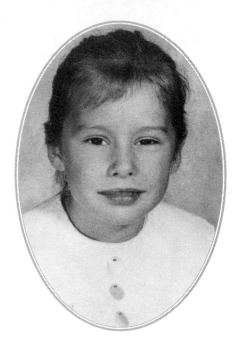

Blessed child held near my heart.

—From A Mother's Memories, Jane Watson Hopping

Spring Song

When the fuzzy pussy willows bud upon the willow tree,
And the tender green of grass-blades cover hill and dale and lea;
When the little birds returning trill with joy and gaily sing,
Then our hearts are full of gladness,
*   For we know that it is spring.*

When the violet and the crocus lift to heav'n their lovely heads,
When little seeds push upward from their warm and earthy beds;
When the lily of the valley all her chime of bells doth ring,
Then our hearts are full of gladness,
*   For we know that it is spring.*

—Alice C. D. Riley

Jane Watson Hopping

Sunlight Breaking Through

When the roosters greet the dawn, and the sun warms the daffodils, our children have always wanted to run out onto the farm and check for baby ducks or geese.

When Colleen was little, she adopted several white hatchling ducks. She couldn't have been a more loving mother. One day I asked her, "If you are a duckling's mother, am I its grandmother?" She laughed and put little Quacker and Waddles back in the nest.

In short months, her very favorite duck followed her all about the place, and soon, as she ran here and there, he began to fly at her shoulder. If she ran down to catch the school bus, he would fly down with her, and when she left, fly home. In the late afternoon, he would be waiting for her to get off the bus, and as she ran up the driveway home, he would again fly along with her.

They were a sight to see! A wonder! A bonding between one of God's creatures and a very small girl.

197

Aunt Esther's Whole-Wheat Bread

MAKES 2 LOAVES

By the thirties, most of the women in the family were baking with store-bought whole-wheat flour. When Mother was a young woman, however, Aunty still made bread with stone-ground flour. Farmers who raised their own grain took it to a local mill to have it ground. Sometimes they paid to have it ground, sometimes they traded. Therefore, the mill usually had some stone-ground flour on hand to sell to people who lived in the community.

2 tablespoons granulated yeast	2 tablespoons salt
1/4 cup warm water (105° to 115°F)	2 beaten eggs
1 tablespoon sugar	5 1/2 to 6 cups whole-wheat flour, plus
2 cups milk	1/2 cup or more unbleached all-
1/4 cup (1/2 stick) butter	purpose flour for kneading and
1/4 cup sorghum or honey	handling

Soften the yeast in the warm water; stir in the sugar. In a small to medium saucepan, warm the milk and then add the butter, sorghum, and salt and stir until the butter is melted and sorghum dissolved. When lukewarm, add the beaten eggs and the yeast mixture. Stir in 2 cups of the whole-wheat flour and beat well. Cover and set the sponge in a warm place to rise.

When puffy on top and light throughout, preheat the oven to 400°F. Add the rest of the flour and stir into a thick dough. Turn dough out onto a flat surface that has been thoroughly coated with all-purpose flour and kneed into a soft, elastic ball.

Cut dough in half and shape into two portions. Pat out into rectangles; roll each rectangle up jelly-roll style. Pinch the sides and ends together. Place top side up in two heavily greased and floured 4-by-8-inch bread pans. Grease the tops of the loaves and bake for 30 minutes, then turn temperature down to 350°F and continue baking until brown, about 35 minutes more. Watch closely at the end of the baking time, because sorghum or honey brown more quickly than sugar. Tap the loaves on the bottom to be certain they sound hollow. Remove from oven, let set in pans 8 to 10 minutes, then turn onto a wire rack to cool.

VARIATION: Pinch the dough into egg-size buns and bake crowded in a well-greased pan with 2- or 3-inch sides. Bake 25 to 35 minutes. Makes 18 to 24 rolls.

Ada's Cider and Tea Punch

MAKES ABOUT 8 CUPS

When I was growing up, this easy-to-make punch was often served at social functions. Women of that day thought it was good for both adults and children.

1 cup orange juice, strained
1/4 cup lemon juice, strained
2 cups sweet cider

2 cups cold ginger ale
4 cups cold tea
Sugar to taste

In a quart container, combine orange juice, lemon juice, and cider and chill thoroughly. When ready to serve, pour into a medium punch bowl. Add cold ginger ale and cold tea and sweeten to taste. Serve at once.

Uncle Leo's Old-Country Pork and Cabbage

MAKES 4 TO 6 SERVINGS

Aunt Esther and Uncle Leo lived on an old farmstead in Missouri. Theirs was a bounteous, self-sufficient wonderland. Mother recalls with pleasure visiting during the various harvest seasons. All through the house, sheds, and barns, food was stored for the winter. When the harvest was in, late in November, the family celebrated at Uncle Leo's house with great potluck suppers.

Mother remembers that first one of the women and then another would set dates for the next get-togethers.

1 medium head fresh cabbage	1/3 cup finely chopped red bell pepper
2 tablespoons butter or margarine	2 cups peeled, seeded, and chopped
2 tablespoons olive oil	fresh tomatoes or whole canned
1 1/2 pounds lean pork, boned and cubed	tomatoes
3/4 cup finely chopped yellow winter onion	1/2 teaspoon thyme or oregano
1 medium clove garlic, mashed	Salt and freshly ground black pepper

Finely shred the cabbage and set aside.

Heat butter and oil in a large heavy skillet over medium-high heat. Turn pork cubes into the skillet and lightly brown the meat. Then remove cubes of pork with a slotted spoon, set aside, and cover to keep warm. Add the onion, garlic, and red pepper to the skillet and cook until soft, stirring frequently but taking care not brown. Add the tomatoes and thyme and season to taste with salt and pepper.

Return pork to frying pan. Cover and simmer for about 30 minutes, stirring occasionally (pork must be cooked well-done). Add shredded cabbage and cook, uncovered, stirring constantly, until cabbage is crisp-tender, 5 to 10 minutes. Serve immediately with Aunt Esther's Whole-Wheat Bread (page 198).

Jane Watson Hopping

Spring weather.

The Pioneer Lady's Hearty Winter Cookbook

In the Folds of the Mountain

Spring comes early to the valley.
The seasons climb backward, up the mountain
where winter holds, with shrinking white fingers
the last of its memories, at the top of the world.

Listen. Do you hear sleigh bells
in the break and tumble of icicles?
Voices and laughter of our earlier selves
beside the bonfire at the skating lake
echo in distant, alpine shadows.
We spent the winter beside the fire
warmed in the company of one another,
sharing hot soup and snow ice cream,
songs and stories and crystal dreams.
Now, spring comes early to the valley
and winter sleeps in the folds of the mountain.
Beneath the greening of timid grass
seeds and new roots stir toward summer,
and snowflakes.

—Alvin Reiss

202

Jane Watson Hopping

The First Day of Spring

Spring has come at last. Warmer nights are soft and wet, blanketed by softly falling rain. At daylight, songbirds fill the air with cheer. Old Man Winter seems on the wane. Young and old frolic in the wet grass and leap fences with gladness in their hearts. Peas are up; Swiss chard has survived the winter.

Girls in pastel colors rival the beauty of crocuses, tulips, and daffodils, which are unfurling to greet the sun. The earth has prepared itself for new life. And we, more a part of nature than we suspect, bask in the sun and wait for a sense of renewal to wash over us!

Daffodils Unfurled

Dear little Daffy-down-dilly
First flow'r of the spring,
Dancing away with the breezes,
Gladness and sunshine you bring.

Daring the cold of the March winds,
Braving the frosts and the snows,
Filling the woods with your glory,
Loveliest flow'r that blows.

—DAFFY-DOWN-DILLY, Alice C. D. Riley

During the Depression of the 1930s, our parents took us to see Daffodil Hill, a showplace, a sight one can never quite forget. The morning was a bit chilly. The sun, thin and creamy yellow, cast its light over the showy daffodil beds. Some contained large, rich yellow flower heads, others small ones with a creamy throat. Our mother said to our father, "I have never seen so many varieties in my life." Daddy then, spending the few coins that he had in his pocket, bought three nodding daffodils, one for Mother and one each for Sheila and me.

Jane Watson Hopping

Mother's California Corn Chowder

Grandpa loved corn chowder. In the winter, when fresh corn was not available, he talked Mother into making up her own recipe out of canned corn.

MAKES ABOUT
6 SERVINGS

$^1/_2$ pound lean bacon, diced
1 medium winter cooking onion, peeled and chopped (about $^1/_2$ cup)
$^1/_2$ cup chopped celery, including celery tops
2 tablespoons all-purpose flour
4 cups (1 quart) milk

1 17-ounce-can cream-style corn
1 pound potatoes, peeled, cooked, and diced
$^1/_2$ teaspoon salt
Pinch of freshly ground black pepper
2 sprigs parsley, snipped, for garnish
Paprika, for garnish

In a large saucepan, fry bacon until crisp; drain off fat and remove bacon from pan. Leave only 3 tablespoons of drippings in the pan. Add onion and celery. Cook and stir until onion is clear and tender.

Remove from heat. Blend the flour into the onion-celery mixture. Return to heat and cook over low heat until mixture is bubbly. Remove from heat; stir in the milk. Stirring constantly, heat to boiling. Boil, stirring, 1 minute. Stir corn, potatoes, salt, and pepper into the chowder and heat through. Stir in the reserved bacon. Serve in deep soup bowls, garnished with minced parsley and paprika.

Easy-to-Make Cheese and Caraway Seed Batter Rolls

These are simple rolls, easy to make, just perfect for young cooks. Effie was the first woman in our family to add grated cheese and caraway seed to the recipe for batter rolls.

MAKES 1 DOZEN
OR MORE

1 tablespoon granulated yeast	2 tablespoons sugar
1¼ cups warm water (105° to 115°F)	2 teaspoons salt
2 tablespoons butter or margarine, melted, plus 2 tablespoons cold butter or margarine for greasing baked rolls	1 cup shredded sharp Cheddar cheese
	1 teaspoon caraway seed
	2 cups all-purpose flour

Set out and thoroughly grease a 12-cup muffin pan.

In a large bowl, dissolve the yeast in the warm water. Add the 2 tablespoons butter and the sugar, salt, cheese, and caraway seed. Blend flour into liquid mixture. Beat by hand or with electric mixer until a smooth batter is formed. Scrape batter from sides of bowl. Cover and let rise in a warm place until doubled in bulk, about 30 minutes.

Stir down batter and beat about 3 minutes. Spoon evenly into prepared pans. Smooth out batter by patting with floured fingertips. Cover and let rise until doubled in bulk, about 40 minutes.

Preheat oven to 375°F. Bake rolls until they are well risen and golden brown and sound hollow when tapped on the bottom. Remove from oven. While still hot, rub cold butter or margarine over tops. Remove from pan and let cool on a wire rack.

Jane Watson Hopping

Aunt Mabel's Dutch Apple Pie with Lemon Pastry

Our great-grandmother was Pennsylvania Dutch. During her younger years she learned from many women how to bake, roast meat, make sauerkraut, and cure meat. Her skills were many! And she taught them to her grandchildren, particularly Aunt Mabel and Mother.

MAKES ONE 9-INCH PIE

Lemon Pastry for Two-Crust Pie
(recipe follows)
5 cups pared and thinly sliced apples
1/2 cup all-purpose flour
3/4 cup sugar
1/2 teaspoon ground cinnamon
1/2 teaspoon grated nutmeg
Dash of salt
1 tablespoon butter or margarine
1/2 cup heavy cream

Preheat oven to 425°F. Set out a 9-inch pie pan. Prepare pastry.

Line the pie pan with half the pastry. Roll out the top crust and dust it with a little flour. Turn apples into a medium bowl. Sift flour with sugar, cinnamon, nutmeg, and salt. Fold into the apples. Turn apple filling into pastry-lined pan. Dot with butter. Cover with top crust. Seal and flute. With a sharp knife, cut extra-large slits in the crust, or using a very small fancy cookie cutter, cut decorative shapes into the top crust.

Bake pie at 425°F for 15 minutes. Then turn down the heat to 350°F and continue baking for 45 more minutes. Five minutes before the pie is completely baked, pour the cream through the slits in top crust. Bake 5 minutes more. Serve warm.

Lemon Pastry for Two-Crust Pie MAKES ONE 9-INCH PIE

2 cups all-purpose flour
1 teaspoon salt
3/4 cup (1 1/2 sticks) butter (no substitute), cubed

1 tablespoon strained lemon juice
1/3 cup water, as needed

Into a medium bowl, sift flour and salt together. Turn butter into flour mixture. Using your fingertips, work butter into the flour until granules the size of peas are formed. Combine lemon juice and water and sprinkle over the flour mixture. Stir with a fork until a cohesive dough ball is formed.

Jane Watson Hopping

The Open Fire

As I sit before the open fire,
    Some thoughts do visit me
Of brownies and the fairies
    And the mermaids of the sea.

And they stand before me waving,
    Then they quickly float away;
Soon I hear them up the chimney,
    And this is what they say:

"Oh, we belong to the open fire—
    A life which is gay and free;
We pass our days in the flames so bright;
    Oh! come, oh, come with me."

—Margaret Stevens (age 10)

Snowflakes, Effie's Faerie Chocolate, and Sitting by the Fire

On cold, wintry days, Grandpa, Mother, Sheila, and I, and Aunt Hattie and our cousins Joan, Pat, and Billie Sue would sit by the fire and watch the sparks fly up the chimney. Those were wonderful days, filled with stories told by Aunt Mabel about faeries and brownies, about snowflake princesses and other magic things. Grandpa would listen, filling his old pipe with homegrown tobacco, and tell wild hunting tales of his youth. As the afternoon waned, he would talk tenderly about living in a small cabin in the woods with his bride, our grandmother, Sitha Jane, and the houseful of young 'uns they brought into this world. He would get quite sentimental when he talked about Myrtle, Maude, and little Ernest, whom they had lost. Then he would recall all the healthy children, those that had lived strong, full lives, and the grandchildren that had brought love and cheer into his life. He would build to a rally, and it would seem as though he had come back to us, to the Hubbard Place in California, and had left his past, for a time, in Missouri.

Jane Watson Hopping

Dreamy Moments, Ancient Longings

Faerie land, once so well known to all, still is a lovely, enchanting place, where tiny, graceful, delicate imaginary beings in human form sing songs, fall in love, and work their magic, taking little notice of mankind. When the moon is high and full, they dance through the night on grasses green, stomping their feet, laughing and shouting until a circle of contrasting colors is formed.

With the light of day, and when the moon is pale, country folk, lying safe in their cots, tell one another stories about the little folk's magic powers. They tell tales about faeries and giants. Sometimes, in midwinter, when the fires are burning brightly, they swear that tiny flitting forms dance in their flickering fires.

Effie's Faerie Chocolate

(This is an antique recipe)

~

MAKES 4 TO 6
SERVINGS

Effie loved to make fancy things, like this chocolate drink, and generously passed her recipes around.

On cold, storming days, when rain and snow fell mixed to the ground, the women in our family often served Effie's delicious old-time chocolate. Needless to say, we children loved this fancy treat.

~

For every 6 tablespoons grated unsweetened chocolate, allow 1 pint boiling water and 4 tablespoons sugar. Mix the chocolate to a paste, with cold water to moisten. Take from the fire and beat with an egg beater, adding by degrees a pint of boiling hot milk, beating all the time. Put into double boiler to keep hot.

Beat a pint of heavy cream until firm and the whites of 3 eggs until dry, then beat into the egg whites $1/3$ cup powdered sugar, and gradually fold in half of the stiff cream. Mix the remaining half of stiff cream with the hot chocolate, and add 1 teaspoonful vanilla.

When serving, fill heavy glasses almost full with hot chocolate, and top each with a tablespoonful of cream. Garnish with candied fruit.

Jane Watson Hopping

All the Loving Homefolk

All through the thirties, our clannish family cared for one another, shared, and saw to it that we children did not fearfully face the times, with all the tragedies that we could not help but see about us.

Mother, Aunt Mabel, Grandpa, and Daddy were pillars of strength that supported our lives. Using their old-time Missouri survival skills, they saw to it that we had adequate clothes, food, care, and love. Aunt Hattie and Mother alternately cared for all five of us little girls, cousins all.

Aunt Irene and Aunt Pauline, who had no children, brought bits of joy into our lives: a bottle of real cologne or lavender-scented toilet water, colorful note paper and thank-you cards.

The Lean Years

On wet, rainy days in spring, women in our families got together to plan large family potlucks. They were sure to invite all their old friends, like Aunt Fanny and Uncle John. Men and boys talked the women into making large pots of soup and pans of hot corn bread. Sometimes women and girls made a raisin pie or a batch of oatmeal cookies.

Most often, meals were simple. Families brought whatever they had to share: simple pots of beans with or without meat in them, split peas, and mashed, scalloped, and baked potatoes. Some brought home-canned tomatoes and fruit. Those were lean times. Grandpa called those midwinter months the Time of Want.

Jane Watson Hopping

Mother's California Bean Soup

MAKES 6 SERVINGS

In the thirties, Mama worked hard milking her cows and tending her chickens, gardening, and home-processing food for us all. She cared for my sister and me, and shared her home with her father. The times for us would have been much different if it had not been for the cohesiveness of our big family. What saved us from the hard times, many felt, was their many life-preserving skills and attitudes.

In winter, we sometimes ate Mother's California Bean Soup, sweet home-churned butter, and her delicious corn bread—for which we counted our blessings. If we had any doubts about just how blessed we were, we talked about loving aunts and uncles, the good health of us all, and the full pantry.

1 cup dry pinto beans
2 quarts Homemade Beef Broth (recipe follows)
1 teaspoon salt
1/2 teaspoon freshly ground black pepper

2 tablespoons all-purpose flour
1/4 cup (1/2 stick) butter or margarine
1/4 teaspoon dried oregano, crumbled
2 cups diced cooked lean beef (optional)

In a large saucepan, soak beans overnight in water to cover. The following morning, boil soaked beans and water 10 to 15 minutes. Add beef stock and cook until beans are soft. Rub through sieve to puree. Return to saucepan; reheat.

In a small bowl, mix salt, pepper, and flour into a paste with 2 tablespoons of the butter; add crumbled oregano. Stir until smooth. Add paste to the pureed beans; cook slowly over low heat for 15 minutes, stirring until bean soup is smooth. Add diced beef, if using, and remaining butter and blend well. Serve hot with corn bread.

215

Homemade Beef Broth MAKES 2 QUARTS OR MORE

2 pounds beef, fat removed
1 pound beef bones
1 teaspoon salt
2 small carrots, peeled and cut into 1-inch pieces
1 large onion, peeled, left whole, studded with whole cloves

1 clove garlic, peeled and quartered
Stalk celery, scraped and cut into 1-inch pieces
2 small bay leaves
6 sprigs of parsley
Sprig of thyme

Rinse the meat. Place meat and bones in a large soup kettle. Pour 3 quarts or more cold water over all. Bring to a boil over medium heat. Remove any scum that settles on the surface of the broth. Add salt, carrots, onion, garlic, celery, bay leaves, parsley, and thyme. Return broth to a boil, lower the heat, and simmer slowly, with cover ajar, for about 3 hours. Add water as needed.

When done, remove meat and bones from broth. Let cool until meat can be handled. Remove any remaining fat. Dice lean meat and set aside. Strain hot broth and discard the vegetables and seasoning agents. Set broth in a cool place until a cake of fat firms up on the surface. Remove and discard fat. Two quarts of clear broth will be needed for the recipe above.

NOTE: Serve remaining broth in deep soup bowls, or refrigerate and use in other dishes that call for beef broth.

Old-Time Johnny Cake

MAKES ONE 8-BY-8-BY-2-INCH CAKE

Grandpa used to call this cake a Journey Cake because people would bake several to take on long jaunts. Mother likes this version; she thinks it's fancier and less like old-fashioned Northern corn bread.

1¼ cups sifted flour	1 cup yellow cornmeal
2 teaspoons baking powder	2 eggs, well beaten
1 teaspoon salt	1¼ cups buttermilk
¾ teaspoon baking soda	3 tablespoons butter or margarine, melted
2 tablespoons sugar	

Preheat oven to 425°F. Thoroughly grease an 8-by-8-by-2-inch loaf pan.

Into a large bowl, sift flour a second time with baking powder, salt, soda, and sugar. Add cornmeal and stir to blend. In a small bowl, combine eggs, buttermilk, and melted butter. Make a well in the center of the dry ingredients. Pour liquid ingredients into well and stir until well blended. Turn into prepared pan.

Bake until done, about 40 minutes. Serve piping hot with homemade butter or margarine.

March

Now, after snow
after sun, white slices
hang, crescents of crystal,
melting life
over tender green
and the new brown of earth
awakening after winter.

Easter is in the air.

—Alvin Reiss

Jane Watson Hopping

Spring Breaks at Last

Every spring, country folk clean up about their places. Gardeners prune roses and fruit trees, haul away the brush, and dress the garden areas with a horse manure mulch. Planting time has come. Cold-weather crops—potatoes, cabbages, peas, onions, shallots, beets, and turnips—are planted in frost-free earth.

Baby ducklings, nesting in a damp bed of straw and mud, break out of their shells to run hither and yon while their mother frantically tries to keep them together, safe from predators. When there is a pond on the farm, the whole family of wild mallards, along with the hatchlings, take up residence along the banks, after hiding deep in the reeds.

Sooner than one would think, the racing young test their wings.

The Pioneer Lady's Hearty Winter Cookbook

Winged and Beautiful and Free

Aunt Mabel was at heart a lover of the wild and free. She and I would go out in the spring. We would watch the hatchlings, older and now more colorful, leave the pond. As they sailed overhead, the sunlight reflecting the sheen of their blue-green feathers, they dipped and flapped their wings until they were out of sight.

She and I would then go back into the house, settle down with milk and cookies, and sing the praises of the winged, beautiful, and free.

Jane Watson Hopping

Aunt Irene's Pineapple Ham Patties

MAKES 5 TO 6 PATTIES

Aunt Irene loved to bake a whole ham for wintry Sunday dinners. Out of ground leftover ham, she often made these delicious patties and served baked sweet potatoes and a hearty salad with them.

3 cups ground leftover ham
1/3 cup fine dry bread crumbs
2 tablespoons firmly packed brown sugar

1/8 teaspoon ground cloves
1 egg, lightly beaten
4 canned pineapple rings, cut in half
1/2 cup pineapple juice

Preheat oven to 350°F. Thoroughly grease a 10-by-10-inch baking dish.

In a medium bowl, combine ham, bread crumbs, brown sugar, cloves, and egg. Shape into 5 or 6 patties. Place in prepared baking dish. Arrange pineapple over and around patties as desired, then pour pineapple juice over all. Bake until patties are done, 45 to 50 minutes.

Scalloped Potatoes au Gratin

MAKES 6 TO 8
SERVINGS

After the harvest, the potato house is full of huge red potatoes, which the women of the family cook in every conceivable way. Grandpa's favorite was scalloped potatoes, with or without cheese.

6 large potatoes, boiled, peeled, and thinly sliced
$^1/_2$ teaspoon or more salt, as desired
$^1/_8$ teaspoon freshly ground black pepper
3 teaspoons all-purpose flour, or more

3 tablespoons butter, or more
$^3/_4$ cup fresh bread crumbs
1 cup grated Swiss cheese
1 cup scalded milk

Preheat oven to 350°F. Set out and grease an 11-by-7-by-1$^1/_2$-inch baking dish.

Arrange potato slices in layers in prepared baking dish, sprinkling each layer with salt and pepper, 1 teaspoon flour, a few dots of butter, 3 or 4 tablespoons fresh bread crumbs, and about $^1/_3$ cup of the grated cheese. Repeat until all potato slices are used, then sprinkle remaining cheese over top layer. Pour over all enough scalded milk to cover potatoes.

Bake until top is golden brown, 40 to 45 minutes. Serve at once.

Jane Watson Hopping

Easy-to-Make Lemon Pie

MAKES 9 SERVINGS

Mincemeat, apple and lemon pies
cool on the window sills,
Put there by aproned Aunt Bessie who warns
"I've eyes in the back of my head Cousin Bill."

—From TEMPTATION, Patricia Parish Kuhn

3 eggs, beaten to a froth
Juice of 2 lemons, strained
1 cup sugar
1 cup heavy cream

Graham Cracker Piecrust (recipe follows)
1/2 cup or more cracker crumbs, for topping

In a double boiler over hot water, cook eggs, lemon juice, and sugar, stirring occasionally, just until thick; remove from heat and let cool at room temperature. Meanwhile, whip cream without sugar until it forms peaks; fold into cooled lemon base. Pour into Graham Cracker Piecrust and top with reserved graham cracker crumbs. Refrigerate until ready to serve.

Graham Cracker Piecrust
MAKES ENOUGH CRUST FOR ONE 9-INCH PIE

1 1/2 cups graham cracker crumbs (about 20 crackers)
1/4 cup sugar

1/2 cup (1 stick) butter or margarine, melted

In a medium bowl, thoroughly combine crumbs and sugar. Stir in just enough butter to bind the crust. Press mixture firmly into a 9-inch pie pan, lining bottom and sides. Bake at 350°F for 10 minutes, or chill for 20 to 30 minutes.

223

The
New Brown
Earth

Here on the farm, early spring rains fall now gently, now with fury on the fields. The cattle seem to welcome the alternating sunshine and rain. The earth soaks up each drop. Grasses abundantly cover the yards and fields. Violets blanket the ground. Gold and crimson tulips fill the flower beds. Our garden patches, dressed with horse manure in February and early March, leach minerals and salts into the new brown earth.

On sunny days, we prepare the worked ground for planting. Soon peas, carrots, turnips, rutabagas, cabbages, and potatoes will pop through. By St. Patrick's Day, we will all be planting potato sets. To meet the needs of our four families, we will plant four to five 200-foot-long rows of potatoes. As spring passes, we will be planting summer and fall crops as well.

Sometimes when I'm walking through the loose, rich earth, checking the progress of planted seeds and tubers, I can feel my grandfather about me. I can hear him call, "Come into the garden with me, Janie! Be careful! Don't step on the little green babies."

Jane Watson Hopping

Homegrown-Potato Salmon Pie

MAKES 6 SERVINGS

Grandpa loved this quick-to-make main dish. Mama served it often in the thirties, hot and ready to eat, to please her father. We still grow the potatoes and make this old family dish to please all the men in our lives.

16-ounce can pink salmon
2 cups Thick White Sauce (recipe follows)
1 cup fresh garden peas, shelled, cooked until tender, and drained

2 cups mashed potatoes, seasoned with salt and freshly ground black pepper
1 tablespoon butter, or more if desired

Into a medium bowl, drain, bone, and flake salmon. Make the Thick White Sauce and keep it warm.

Preheat oven to 450°F. Fold white sauce and peas into salmon. Turn filling into a medium casserole dish. Top with mashed potatoes and dot with butter. Bake until lightly browned, about 15 minutes.

Serve with spring vegetables and follow with spring fruits.

Thick White Sauce   MAKES ABOUT 2 CUPS

¹/₂ cup (1 stick) butter or margarine
¹/₂ cup all-purpose flour
¹/₂ teaspoon salt
¹/₄ teaspoon freshly ground white
   pepper (black pepper can be
   substituted)

2 cups milk (or 1 cup milk and 1 cup
  light cream)

Melt butter in a saucepan over low heat. Blend in flour, salt, and pepper.
Cook over low heat until mixture is smooth and bubbly. Remove from heat.
Stir in milk. While stirring constantly, heat the sauce to boiling. Continue
boiling and stirring for 1 minute longer.

On an April Day

Birds on the boughs before the buds
Begin to burst in Spring,
Bending their heads to the April floods,
Too much out of breath to sing.
O' the warm, delicious, hopeful rain!
Let us be glad together.
Summer comes flying in beauty again,
Through the fitful April weather.

—Celia Thaxter

Jane Watson Hopping

Mingled Sunshine and Rain

Changeable April, known for its varied weather—unannounced rain, sunshine, frost, and snow! These bouts of weather seldom last long. In the woods and across the fields, buds of trees, bushes, and flowers burst open, creating a pastel wonderland. Grasses grow richly green; small animals come out of their burrows. The woods are alive with flocks of birds that have flown in from the South. Soon nests will be filled with fledglings. Butterflies flit from blossom to blossom, drinking in sweet nectar. Bees, not to be outdone, go about the serious task of gathering honey for winter from wildflowers, daffodils, crocuses, and snowdrops.

The Laughter of April Rills

There's beauty in the lilac scent
That haunts the breath of spring;
There's beauty in the miracles
That changing seasons bring.

—BEAUTY, Priscilla May Moore

In April, God's creatures are athrill to the wakening of spring. Icy rivulets

scamper down hill and dale. The scent of blooming orchards, wild trees,

and shrubs fills the air, proclaiming this wonder-working season. Budding

daffodils capture the senses. Nesting robins speak of rebirth.

The natural world struts its stuff!

Jane Watson Hopping

Roast Spareribs
Country Style

〜

In the spring, Ada's menfolk butchered and sold their young pigs. Grandpa always bought one, and so did Floyd, who then shared with Aunt Clary. Mother, who loved pork, thought it was the winter apples fed out of storage to the hogs that made the meat so tender and sweet.

2 pounds spareribs
Salt and freshly ground black pepper
1 cup fine, dry bread crumbs

$1/4$ teaspoon dried thyme, crumbled
1 tablespoon minced onion

Preheat the oven to 350°F. Place ribs in a shallow baking dish; sprinkle with salt and pepper. Put the dish into a greased brown paper bag and roast for 45 minutes, then remove dish from bag and continue roasting, uncovered, for an additional 45 minutes.

Mix bread crumbs with thyme and onion. Just before taking meat from oven, sprinkle bread crumb mixture over spareribs. Baste ribs with pan drippings and return to oven until crumbs are brown, about 5 minutes.

Serve piping hot with Quick-and-Easy Mashed Potato Balls (recipe follows).

Quick-and-Easy Mashed Potato Balls

MAKES 6 SERVINGS

Grandpa loved red potatoes. Every year on St. Patrick's Day, he planted potato sets, enough so that there would be a generous crop. By late August, he would dig as many as 1,600 pounds and share them with those in the family who had a poor crop or no potatoes at all.

3 cups cold mashed potatoes
1 egg yolk

Salt and freshly ground black pepper
Butter

Preheat oven to 425°F. Thoroughly grease a medium baking sheet and set aside.

In a medium to large bowl, combine mashed potatoes, egg yolk, salt, and pepper. Shape potato mixture into 6 balls. Place balls in the prepared pan, make a depression in the top of each, and put a bit of butter in the depression. Bake until lightly browned. Serve piping hot.

Jane Watson Hopping

Grandpa's Favorite Raisin-Pecan Batter Bread

~

MAKES 2 LOAVES

Mother doesn't remember where Grandpa got the pecans for this bread, but she thinks some of Uncle Joe's children might have sent them to him from Missouri or Texas.

1 cup milk
1/2 cup light honey
1/2 cup (1 stick) butter or margarine, softened at room temperature
1 teaspoon salt
2 tablespoons granulated yeast

1/2 cup warm water (105° to 110°F)
2 eggs, lightly beaten
5 cups all-purpose flour
1 cup golden raisins
1 cup coarsely chopped pecan meats

Thoroughly grease two 9-by-5-by-3-inch loaf pans; set in a cool place until needed.

If using raw milk, scald it in a small saucepan over medium heat, then turn off heat. Add honey, butter, and salt; stir until butter is melted and honey and salt are dissolved. Let cool to lukewarm.

In a large bowl, dissolve yeast in warm water; let sit until frothy, about 10 minutes. Stir in the milk mixture, eggs, and 2 cups of the flour. Beat until smooth. Add remaining flour gradually until a stiff dough is formed. Cover and let rise until doubled in bulk, 45 minutes to 1 hour. (To test, touch the dough. If an impression remains when touched, the dough has doubled in bulk.) Preheat oven to 350°F during the last 15 to 20 minutes of rising time. When well risen, stir down the dough. Add raisins and pecans and stir to incorporate. Then turn dough into prepared loaf pans.

Bake until bread is well risen, firm to the touch, and golden brown, 40 to 45 minutes. When done, remove bread from oven and immediately turn out of pans onto a wire rack. Set the loaves top side up and grease lightly with a little butter or margarine. Let cool to room temperature.

The Fairy Flower

Deep in the shadow of the wood,
With somber things around it,
The little fairy flower stood,
And a little maiden found it.
She found it on a dreary day
When, for some mournful reason,
The blue sky seemed not blue, but gray,
And life a lonesome season.

But when she plucked it from the bed
Where nothing matched its whiteness,
The fairy blossom seemed to shed
A sudden lovely brightness.
As though it had some happy art
To reach the springs of gladness,
It comforted her heavy heart
And charmed away her sadness.

The little maiden cherished it,
And henceforth in her bosom,
As something dear and delicate,
She hid the fairy blossom.
It never lost its subtle charm
To overcome vexations
And take the sting from every harm,
Because its name was—Patience!

—Mary Bradley

232

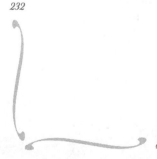

Jane Watson Hopping

Unfolding Gladness

Shortly before Easter, our family would go up into the hills of Eldorado County for a picnic. The men set up tables and benches and the women spread blankets to sit on or to pull up around us if the spring air was a bit chilly.

One of our favorite picnic spots was among the remains of what had been a thriving pioneer homestead. The shakes on the old barn roof had held fast for who knows how many years. Yellow roses bloomed where porches had once been. Hitching posts, handmade on a blacksmith's forge, waited for horses that no longer came.

By noon everyone was fam-ished. While the men played a game of catch, Mama, Aunt Mabel, Aunt Irene, and Aunt Pauline set out the food. Aunt Fanny and Uncle John, who were both older than

Uncle Charlie, Chris, and Rachel

233

Grandpa, sat in chairs they had brought with them and waited for a call to dinner.

Ours was a family of cut-ups, and spring brought out the best antics. Uncle Ben recited riddles, and everyone laughed and told stories, sang silly songs, and teased everyone else. After dinner, our fathers and uncles would chase us and grab us and swing us around, while mothers and aunts said things like "Don't tear her dress," or "You are making her ribbons fall out!"

Later in the day, everyone was ready for a long nature walk in the woods. Aunt Mabel loved the blooming wildflowers, and moss-hung trees, springs, and creeks. She would take us children with her to nature's treasure trove of wild iris, lilies, and more. Her gift was indeed a celebration of spring.

Jane Watson Hopping

Spinach and Ham Salad Garnished with Deviled Eggs

~

MAKES 6 SERVINGS

Old-time farm women always had a small flock of laying hens. They generously used the eggs at home and sold the oversupply to obtain pin money, which they usually stashed in a sugar bowl.

2 cups spinach, steamed until tender
Salt and freshly ground black pepper
Juice of 1 lemon
6 Deviled Eggs (recipe follows)
At least 6 lettuce leaves (red leaf
   preferred)

6 slices cold boiled ham (about
   ³/₈ inch thick)
Any dressing desired

Drain spinach and season with salt, pepper, and lemon juice. Pack spinach into 6 small molds. Chill. Meanwhile, prepare Deviled Eggs. Chill.

Just before serving, cover platter with lettuce leaves. Place ham in center of platter. Garnish with molded spinach and Deviled Eggs. Serve cold with dressing of choice.

Deviled Eggs   MAKES 6 SERVINGS

6 eggs
Mayonnaise
Salt and freshly ground black pepper
   to taste

Lemon juice to taste
Paprika

Wash eggs. Cover with boiling water. Simmer 25 to 30 minutes. Remove from water. Quickly immerse in cold water. Peel, then cut eggs in half lengthwise. Remove yolks, mash, and moisten with mayonnaise until filling is creamy. Season to taste with salt, pepper, and lemon juice. Mix until light and fluffy. Pile lightly into egg whites. Dust with paprika.

Aunt Irene's Stuffed Figs

MAKES 6 OR 8
STUFFED FIGS

Aunty served this confectionlike dish after dinner with coffee for grown-ups and milk for us.

$^1/_2$ pound golden figs
   Maraschino cherries, 2 cherries for
      each fig
   Slivered almonds, 5 slivers to each fig

$^1/_4$ cup orange juice
2 teaspoons lemon juice
3 tablespoons sugar

Stuff each fig with 2 whole cherries and insert almond slivers around cherries. In a small saucepan, combine orange juice, lemon juice, and sugar. Add figs, cover, and simmer until figs are tender. Drain, let cool, and serve on a small plate from which each person at the table serves himself or herself.

Jane Watson Hopping

Shrove Tuesday

The name Shrove Tuesday originated from the old custom of confession to and absolution by a priest (receiving shrift) on the day before Lent. Traditionally, in many countries and communities, the day is one of celebration and rejoicing. It is the Carnevale of the Italians, the Mardi Gras of the French, and the Pancake Day of the English.

Aunt Alice, English to the core, insisted Mama and sister and I celebrate Pancake Day with her.

Pancake Day

When the sun rose on Shrove Tuesday, Aunt Alice, like other country folk of English descent, celebrated age-old Pancake Day with fervor.

On this holiday, English women and girls often competed to see who could bake the largest pancake, throw it up into the air, and catch it on the griddle on its way down in the same flipping motion we use when making flapjacks.

Among the many other customs celebrating this holiday, there are the Lemon Fight, the Goose March, Lent Crocking, and Football Contests, many of which are enlivened by games with jingling rhymes of little reason.

Jane Watson Hopping

Quick-and-Easy Pancakes

MAKES 4 TO 6
PANCAKES

Both Sheila and I learned to make pancakes on a griddle or in Mama's heavy cast-iron frying pan. Mama taught us that all batters contain fat, which keeps them from sticking, and that all batters should be cooked over low heat. She showed us how to test the griddle or frying pan by sprinkling a little cold water on the heated surface: if it danced about, the pan or griddle was hot enough.

Such cakes, she told us, are supposed to be dry and not grease-soaked.

$1^1/_2$ cups all-purpose flour
$2^1/_2$ teaspoons baking powder
2 tablespoons sugar
$^3/_4$ teaspoon salt

2 eggs
1 cup milk
$^1/_4$ cup ($^1/_2$ stick) butter, melted

Into a medium mixing bowl, sift flour with baking powder, sugar, and salt. In a smaller bowl, whip the eggs, milk, and butter together. Make a well in the center of the flour mixture, then pour the egg-milk mixture into the flour mixture, working the batter just until the dry ingredients are thoroughly incorporated.

Heat and lightly grease the griddle. Pour or spoon batter onto prepared griddle or into lightly greased iron skillet to make 4- to 6-inch pancakes. Cook one pancake at a time, leaving space to turn it over. Cook over low heat until the bottom side is golden brown and the top of the pancake is full of holes formed by bubbles that rise and break. Turn only once. Serve with syrup, jam, or jelly.

NOTE: Undercooking yields a soggy pancake, and overcooking yields one on which the crust is too brown and tough.

To make a thinner batter, add $^1/_4$ to $^1/_2$ cup more milk; to make a richer batter, add an extra egg. For variety, drop the batter by the spoonful onto the griddle to make silver-dollar pancakes, or add $^1/_2$ cup blueberries, dried fruit, bits of crisp fried bacon, or small cubes of ham to the batter.

A Grandma's Dream

Young Melinda's Grandma Hatch was a lovely, creative, talented woman who held the little ones on her lap while she read and told wonderful stories to them all. Sometimes, she stood before them reading and dramatizing bits of her favorite poetry.

Melinda's favorite was a delightful story about a whistling boy. Now grown up with a family of her own, she fondly recalls those early days and fervently hopes to find among family papers a yellowed sheet on which is penned a story about a whistling boy, authored by Elizabeth Gladys Hatch.

Jane Watson Hopping

Grandma Hatch's Ginger Cookies
(An old-time recipe)

MAKES ABOUT 36 COOKIES

On spring days, when the weather was warming up and leaves were budding out, and flowers once again were gracing the earth, Grandma Hatch baked a batch or two of ginger cookies and served them to family, neighbors, and friends, along with hot coffee and icy milk.

$^3/_4$ cup Crisco or other vegetable shortening

1 cup sugar, plus $^1/_2$ cup for dipping tops of cookies

1 egg, beaten to a froth

$^1/_4$ cup molasses

2 cups all-purpose flour

$1^1/_2$ teaspoons baking soda

$1^1/_2$ teaspoons ground cinnamon

$1^1/_2$ teaspoons ground ginger

$^1/_2$ teaspoon salt

Preheat oven to 350°F. Set out a large baking sheet.

In a large bowl, cream together shortening and the 1 cup sugar. Blend in egg and molasses. Into a medium bowl, sift flour with baking soda, cinnamon, ginger, and salt. Stir flour mixture into the liquid ingredients. Cover dough and leave in refrigerator long enough to firm up the dough, 15 minutes or longer. When firm, remove dough from refrigerator and shape into 36 balls; dip the top of each ball in sugar, place on cookie sheet, and flatten with a fork. Bake until risen and lightly browned, 12 to 15 minutes.

The Lord Is Risen

In the still, gray dawn, through dew-hung grass
They sought the sepulcher, silent, alone,
Their spirits troubled with this one thought:
"Oh, who shall roll us away the stone?"

But the gray dawn fled before the light
That gleamed from a seraph's radiant face,
And blossoms sprang from his footprints when
He swung the stone from its resting place.

The grass that was lately cold and wet
Sparkled and glowed in the dawn's gold spray;
An anthem echoed from far-off heights;
"The Lord! the Lord is risen today!"

—Jessie Wilmore Murton, *Best Loved Unity Poems*

Jane Watson Hopping

Oh, Who Shall Roll Us Away the Stone?

On Easter Sunday, Christian churches commemorate the resurrection of our Lord the Christ. This religious holiday may come as early as March 22 or as late as April 25. Easter marks the end of Lent, the period of fasting and social retirement. Society generally unites with the church in making Easter a special holy day. White lilies, signifying purity and resurrection, are given to friends and family, and large baskets of lilies grace the churches of the land.

Women deck themselves out in spring-like dresses and hats, and men put on their best, the new clothes representing the return of spring. Some join a small-town parade.

God Bless the Children

Soon our Hannah will share her third birthday with us. Naomi, age four, will help her sister Rachel and her mother, Lisa, with napkins and cups and picking up colored paper. Sometimes, when I look at them, with their golden and red-gold hair and the loving smiles on their faces, I know without any doubt that God in his loving kindness has given them to us for a while, to shelter and love.

Jane Watson Hopping

Beloved Daughters

During this holy time of year, I am reminded that my husband and I have had the privilege of knowing our first two daughters, Amy Lynne Maddox and Janet Charlen Christman, to have heard their voices in song, to have seen the talents and skills they were given. And to know their love. It comforts us to know that they are with God.

Each year, along with spring blossoms, comes the reminder of their beauty, their shining golden hair, their laughter. The hopes we had for them, our love for them. Amy just a child, and Janet a brilliant young woman, both succumbed to cancer.

It's a time when we, the family, feel particularly vulnerable and close-knit.

Prayer for a Very New Angel

Give her kind deeds to do
Small tasks to share—
And may she heed those precious childhood graces;
For just to have her presence there
Must set a smile upon the Angels' faces.
Please give her playmates, Lord,
This joyous child
Sweet cherubs filled with song
And loving laughter
But just to let her know
You need her there,
Lord, yet some need a little looking after.
The years she paused with us
Were all too brief,
Yet filled with joy enough to offset grief
Oh! Angels who again have learned to smile—
Thank you for sharing her this little while!

—Lois Adams, grandmother

Jane Watson Hopping

Index

247

Jane Watson Hopping

Jane Watson Hopping

Jane Watson Hopping

253

Jane Watson Hopping

Jane Watson Hopping

R

Q

S

About the Author

JANE WATSON HOPPING, author of *The Pioneer Lady's Country Kitchen, The Pioneer Lady's Country Christmas, The Country Mothers Cookbook, The Lazy Days of Summer Cookbook,* and *The Many Blessings Cookbook,* loves her quiet country life on a homestead in Oregon, enjoying gardening and the natural beauty that surrounds her.